# Fashion Fables

# Fashion Fables

*Inside the Business of Fashion*

**ANINDYA RAY**

DIGITALSPINES

First Edition, 2023



Paperback ISBN: 978-81-976876-2-4
eBook ISBN: 978-81-19316-21-2
WebPDF ISBN: 978-81-19316-22-9



Published by DIGITAL SPINES.
Originally published by 16Leaves.

Printed and bound in India.

# Contents

# Foreword

Life is a journey – one laden with ups & downs, learnings & lessons, experiences & anecdotes… And to be able to share them with the world is a rewarding experience, something that I have been thinking of doing for a long, long time.

My writing journey started during the pandemic, when I finally put pen to paper and started developing a chapter on insideapparel.net.

Initially, I strung together a few words, out of the massive archive of my learnings & experiences from the Indian Fashion industry, but today, those chapters have taken the shape of this book.

I wanted to write not because I am a wordsmith, but because I wanted to share my learnings with others, in the hope that it will help them navigate this ever-changing fashion industry.

In this industry, there is no formula for success and, most of the times, 1+1 is not 2. Nonetheless, experiences help you navigate these uncertainties better.

**But do you need to make your own mistakes to learn?**

I believe not. For intelligent is the person who can learn from others' mistakes too.

**But how will that happen when no one really writes in this industry?**

Don't get me wrong. There are many books written about the fashion industry but next to none talk about the back end or the unattractive aspects of this industry.

We talk about beautiful designs made by the brands & the designers, but seldom do we speak about the merchandisers who, painstakingly, ensure that the designs reach the shop floor for you to buy.

If we look back, in most ancient cultures, lessons were initially passed on verbally for generations and later, at some point, written down; I would like this book to be a start in the furtherance of the written word.

The future professionals need not repeat the mistakes my counterparts & I have made and learnt, that in many ways, shaped the industry the way it is today.

I have been a part of the fashion industry for more than 30 years now and have seen fashion through a completely different lens. For you to understand my writing, learnings and experiences, you must understand what **'Fashion'** really means to me.

To the world it is synonymous with ART; It's a trend and an expression of creativity.

But to me, fashion is nothing but a **'business mechanism'** - one that creates a demand when there is no actual need for it.

Shocking! Isn't it?

But this is the truth.

## A BIT OF HISTORY

Let's deep dive into the history of fashion and analyse how it has worked on the mass psyche and how it dominates and dictates consumerism, forcing unsuspecting people to be a part of this journey of evolving fashion trends.

According to me, fashion, in yesteryears, was about quality, colours and craftsmanship. This, however, had a narrow audience; it was only restricted to the royal or the noble classes. To the masses, clothes were mostly a necessity, something to cover the body with & protect it against weather changes.

Fashion, in those times, was mostly centered around what the human hand could create. It was the artisans that were highly regarded for the skills they possessed - be it the exquisite seamstresses of France or the fine cotton weavers of India.

It's interesting to note, that India was the largest producer and exporter of fine cotton fabric in the 1800's which occupied a 23-25% share of India's GDP. India was renowned for its fine quality & craftsmanship.

But with the passing years, the scenario changed.

## INDUSTRIAL REVOLUTION

The industrial revolution gave rise to '**Fashion Retail**' as we see it today.

It replaced the human hand with machines and started large scale production of fabrics. Lakhs of metres would be produced on these machines, monthly. This led to surplus or excessive production - a much higher supply than there was demand for.

Now, the industrialists, who had heavily invested in setting up of these factories, had to sell their goods failing which they would incur losses. A direct conclusion for this problem was that they needed to create a market for their product. Thus, came in the practice of creating artificial demand in the clothing industry. All thoughts and mechanisms focused on how to make people buy more clothes when they do not even need it.

Seasonal clothing, which was a mere practical need due to shift in weather conditions, became a trend paradigm. The industry started telling people that they need to wear deeper & darker colours during winters and brighter and cheerful ones during summer. The 'chintz pink' from this summer was getting replaced by 'paloma pink' for the next summer. The winter coat from last year became outdated because it was not done in the colour for this year.

Though, largely, a western concept, this seeped into the fashion retail space world over with globalisation. Even in tropical countries, like India, we were made to believe that summer & winter calls for different fabrics, colours and silhouettes.

Slowly, the designers got replaced by big brands, who projected trends for the coming seasons, made millions of pieces, advertised and told people what they need to wear to stay in tune with trends.

Over the many years, fashion became for the masses and a social need to abide by, failing which one would be looked down upon.

So, what started as a demand and supply mechanism by the industrialists became a social dictate of today. Being fashionable became a need. Thereby, buying fashionable clothes became a necessity…

The brands have come up with different creative solutions to ensure they keep selling more & more. Even a sturdy garment like jeans, which is meant to be worn for years, is reinvented every year. The 'mid-rise skinny fit', that was popular two years ago, has now been replaced by the 'high-rise flare fit'. This, clubbed with higher purchasing power of the consumers, has created a new-age phenomenon - one lead by '**Fast Fashion**'.

When I look back at my childhood, I do not remember buying clothes as often as we do now. We mostly bought clothes around festival times or special occasions like a wedding in the family or a birthday.

In fact, we took pride in our 'pass-me-downs'. The clothes passed on from the older to the younger siblings, mom's saree passed on as wedding trousseau or father-in-law's pashmina shawl passed on to the son-in-law, were prized possessions.

Those were the days when fabric was bought and thoughtfully stitched from the neighborhood tailor. After that, ready-made garments came into vogue, permeating the landscape of India and the rest of the globe as well. This, devastatingly, affected the buying pattern of the people. Suddenly, we started producing, buying and wearing clothes that we did not need.

A little bit of research in this context leads us to some shocking revelations.

A typical household in the USA in the 1950's and 1960's used to throw away 12 garments a year, and today that number stands at 65 garments a year, some of which are worn once or never.

Today, fashion has gone beyond clothes and jewellery. Look at mobile phones for an example… and I must admit, I am no less a victim of this!

I remember buying my first iPhone in 2009. Ever since, the world has seen a new iPhone model launch every year and I, myself, have bought a new one every 2 or 3 years, irrespective of the fact that my old iPhone works well, maybe even as efficiently as the newer one, yet I succumb to the idea of having that new phone in my hand. I know many, like me, do succumb to the desire of owning that new piece of technology. Maybe because we feel better. Buying a phone, in today's world, is as important in creating a fashion statement as buying trendy garments.

Gone are the days when the brands divided their calendars into two seasons; today we talk about nimble supply chain, where brands can launch new collections every 15 days, coaxing the customer to buy more and more to stay relevant. They dictate the market by stating, "this autumn these colours of Fall will sell" or "this winter parka or a trench coat or anorak would sell".

Consumers keep coming back trying to find clothes matching the trend and, inevitably, buy. Interestingly, the concept of FOMO (*fear of missing out*) acted as a bigger pull in this scenario.

## THE VILLAINOUS INVENTORY

With the passing of time, the practice of seasonality became the DNA of the fashion industry. At universities, students were taught to work on seasons; professionals were taught to plan such too.

In fact, fashion forecasting agencies are a mainstay of the fashion industry today. Huge amounts of money and time are spent on researching and putting together reports that tell us what is going to sell 2 years from now - the colours, silhouettes, fabrics and more. The designers and buyers base their seasonal work on these predictions.

What we are essentially doing is – '**Forecasting**'. We are creating an inventory basis what will sell 2 years from now and such assumptions.

Based on this, the unique method of '**spray and pray**' came about. Make goods, send it to 200 stores, put up some ads and pray that someone would come and buy those goods.

And this is the **real villain of our industry**!

Inventory eats up the capital in this industry. The brands stock huge inventory in the hope to sell the goods and make money. The problem is that everything is based on prediction and most of us have no clue what will sell.

Many a times, in my experience, our predictions have miserably failed. What we thought would be a hit product turned out to be a failure that forced us to incur losses due to liquidation.

The advent of social media has made this worse. We are in a situation where brands have lost their power to force trends on consumers. Today, consumers make their own trends. It is, after all, the age of the creators and not followers.

Buying behaviour has completely changed and brands, today, are unable to forecast what the consumer will buy and from where. Consumers, who looked at brands for education on fashion trends, are now becoming the educators themselves, defining trends as they go. The forecasting model, in this scenario, is completely out of sync. How can one predict what the consumer will wear 2 years ahead when trends change daily?

This unpredictability of forecast method clubbed with the economies of scale makes inventory the biggest evil of this industry.

So, I ask - does making 5000 pieces of a product make sense?

## RISE OF THE NEW-AGE FASHION BUSINESSES

With the advent of social media and technology, fashion retail has also seen a shift. Most consumers, these days, are purchasing through phones, tablets or laptops from the convenience of their homes. This enables the brands to engage with the consumers on a daily basis. And that's where the new-age, tech-driven fashion brands are breaking the mould. They look at fashion retail very differently.

The hard-coded system of seasons and all, on which the fashion industry is primarily built, does not matter to them.

They have built a new age supply chain where only 50-150 pieces of a style may be manufactured. The images of these are put out on social media and their respective websites. And if they sell, they make more of those - killing the inventory evil and limiting their losses in the form of liquidation and capital that is stuck.

## PUSH-BASED TO PULL-BASED MARKET DYNAMICS

When brands manufacture what is sold, it is called the '**Pull-based Strategy**', which is diametrically opposite to the '**Push-based Strategy**', where the brands decide what to make and push into the market.

In the pull-based strategy, only what's sold is made, reducing the inventory burden to a minimal, thereby reducing the losses for the business. The equation is simple: less inventory equals to less capital invested and less inventory also equals to less liquidation.

The methodology, used by these brands, is simple: hold fabric as inventory, create a sample, showcase to the consumers, and make when the order comes in.

In some cases, the brands choose to make 50-150 pieces in the style and make more of it as the sale happens.

Basically, if there is demand, the brands will supply.

This strategy is further evolving as new-age brands adopt technology to replace the process of creating a sample and doing a photoshoot. They are now creating 3D or virtual models of the garment, putting it up on social media to garner responses and then manufacturing the garments. By doing so, it further reduces the inventory risk and heightens the probability of success.

As the consumers evolve, new technology comes to the forefront and so do, brands and the fashion retail spaces.

In the coming chapters, we will dwell further into these concepts but before doing so, it was imperative to understand what fashion retail really was, is and will be in the future.

Overall, the fashion retail industry has evolved over all these years. But most of these learnings are not written down and passed on. This book is my endeavour to doing so.

## PART 1

# THE FUTURE OF FASHION

***The fashion industry has gone through many changes from time to time... And today it stands on the principle of a metamorphic evolution.***

Gone are the glory days of the 80's and 90's, the new era has brought with itself a new way of life. The advent of technology has changed our lives completely and has impacted how the business of fashion runs. Not just the front end, but also the back end.

Today, every facet in the fashion industry works differently, be it the designers who draw magic with their minds or the manufacturers who make the designers' vision a reality!

This first part - **"The Future of Fashion"** - dwells into the core of the fashion industry and the many functions that run it, while exploring its future.

CHAPTER 1.1

# Future of the Fashion Industry and its Impact

This is the first of the '**Future**' series - a set of 6 articles - where I talk about the **Future of the Fashion Industry and its Impact** on various functions and stakeholders. In this article, I want to discuss the components which are driving the future of fashion from the consumer perspective.

The consumer has been evolving. While the basic product has not changed, a few things that have are:

- Where he/she buys
- Who influences him/her to buy
- How important is fashion to him/her

These last few years have seen a paradigm shift in consumer behaviour while the industry is still playing catch-up. It is still working in the shadow of the 80's & 90's glory days.

Consumers still buy as many clothes if not more, just not as much from the same old established players. Caught up in the idea of forecasting, planning, seasons, trade shows, the fashion industry has been trying to manage the disaggregated stakeholders in the supply chain through the old analog process of mails, excel sheets and endless meetings.

A lot of new companies, who were digital-first and did not understand the rules of the fashion industry, experimented with the idea of a supply chain, and succeeded in changing the very rules of the game. For example, BooHoo, Asos, just to name a few.

First, let's discuss these sweeping changes in the consumer landscape.

## 1. Experience Over Acquisition

Even in the early 2000's, fashion and brands were prized possessions. But now, a lot of that wallet share has moved to acquiring experiences whether it's dining out, holidaying, engaging in online content or gaming. The ability to immortalise people's experiences through social media is making these ways cooler than just being old-school fashionable.

## 2. The Selfish Generation

Decades of peace and development have assured this generation of their financial and physical security. Thus, this new generation is more focused on pursuing their interests and hobbies. This has created the most self-obsessed generation ever and, in return, they are also influencing other generations around them. This has virtually re-written the relevance of fashion in the current generation, where desires have moved beyond acquiring material things.

## 3. The Lazy Economy

There was a time when going out for shopping was a pleasurable use of time. But today, with so much to do and such little time in hand, is going out for shopping as big as it used to be? Even older generations have started buying online. And given India's infrastructure, very few want to brave traffic, parking queues and pollution to go out to shop when they can just easily do it online.

## 4. A Sign From Mother Nature

Almost everyone is enjoying the reduced pollution and stress levels, even the birds have returned to the cities. 'Work from Home' is now a reality which will not only reduce the need for commercial spaces, but also reduce traffic, minimise travel and make people question the old status quo. Sustainability and 'green fashion' are movements that will gain from this awakening as will the renewed advent of slow fashion.

## 5. Sustainable Living

Better awareness of the ecological damages, caused by the fashion industry, is pushing consumers to demand for more sustainable fashion, brands and retailers to care for the world around them. Apparel supply chains have constantly shifted their manufacturing to underdeveloped nations to maintain and reduce costs. Over the last few decades, the inflation of final consumer price in garments is the lowest when compared to all other categories and industries.

This global catastrophe has fast forwarded technology, making work-from-home, disaggregated teams, online meetups, digital economy and virtual living, a reality. So how will this further impact consumer behaviour?

## 6. Living With Less

Suddenly, it has dawned upon people that it's possible to live with less. This thought has brought families together, friends closer and communities first. People are suddenly realising that it's possible to make time for the 'more important' things in life. Marketers may need to work doubly hard on keeping their businesses relevant.

## 7. Need For Security

Need for security will impact the 'where & how' we buy. It may well accelerate e-commerce businesses by a decade, besides also paving a way for collaboration between the online and brick & mortar industries to work with each other. Just like how, today, one may use multiple debit cards of different banks in the same ATM, in the future, all stores may become fulfilment points across channels - paving the way for a seamless consumer experience.

So, what do all these mean for the fashion industry? While a lot of traditional businesses seem to be failing, there are a lot of new players moving from strength to strength.

What are the lessons to be learnt here?

## 8. Fashion Vs. Trends

In these series of articles, for the ease of understanding, the two words have been defined differently. 'Fashion' refers to the ability of brands to dictate what the consumers will wear, while 'Trends' refers to what the consumers prefer to wear. Consumers mix and match to create trends which brands need to recognise and follow.

In the golden age of brands, the 80's, 90's and early 2000's, brands were able to dictate fashion to their consumers. Today, trends are made on social media and are easily available. It is all happening 'right now' and not waiting to be forecast by brands.

### 9. The Consumer Is in The Driver's Seat

This has never been truer. Social Media and E-Commerce have democratised the marketplace. Brands no longer forecast fashion, and designers no longer influence it to the extent they used to. For the first time, since the industrial revolution, the wheel has turned completely. Digital markets have allowed consumers to buy what they want and from whom they want. Brands will find it increasingly difficult to dictate terms to the consumers.

### 10. The Changing Relevance of Brands

Earlier, brands stood for lifestyle niche. Buying the brand meant buying into its philosophy. If you bought a Nike, you bought into its lifestyle. Wearing the brand communicated that you stood for active lifestyle.

But today, all you have to do is post a selfie, sweating it out in the gym, and it sends out the same message.

Brands must engage with their consumers at a much deeper level. The brands need to resonate the consumers' philosophy. Brands, which are unable to do this, run the risk of losing relevance.

We, the insiders of the apparel industry are at the brink of change. To stay relevant, we must innovate processes and think outside the box. And we need to do this today!

**A few fundamental questions that arise are:**

- What is the role of **DESIGN?** Is it just enough to forecast fashion? Do we need to decentralise our teams? Do we need to curate and not just create?

- How will **SUPPLY CHAIN** move from a forecast-based to a demand-driven model? Would this have an impact on the inventory levels? Are small lot sizes really a challenge?
- Can **B&M** afford to look at multiple products as one entity? Do we need to adapt a segmentation strategy to manage product? Can we not apply different rules of demand to different segments?
- Are conventional **MARKETING & SALES** methodologies enough? Do we need to become digital first? Do we need to reimagine offline business too?
- What is the **ROLE OF THE VENDOR** in this new world? Does he become the innovation and trend-spotting lab for the brands?

The following articles will dwell deep into each function and discover the answers to the above questions. Looking forward to your comments. Let's make these conversations as rich as possible.

CHAPTER 1.2

# The Future of Fashion Marketing

This is the second article in the **Future Series**. In the previous article, we discussed the changing consumer behaviour and how it's impacting the industry. In this article, I want to talk about what this means for fashion companies.

In this article, 'Brands' refers to both retail brands and fashion brands.

The one major takeaway we get from this fast-changing consumer behaviour is that brands need to reassess their relevance to their consumers as seen here. In the 80's, 90's and the early 2000's, which I refer to as the Golden Era of Fashion brands, the brand made the person. Now, in this newly established status quo, the brand is trying to fit into the life of the person. People's lifestyles are the biggest decider.

When I look at the Indian market today, it looks like a deluge of opportunism as opposed to well-thought through positioning of brands.

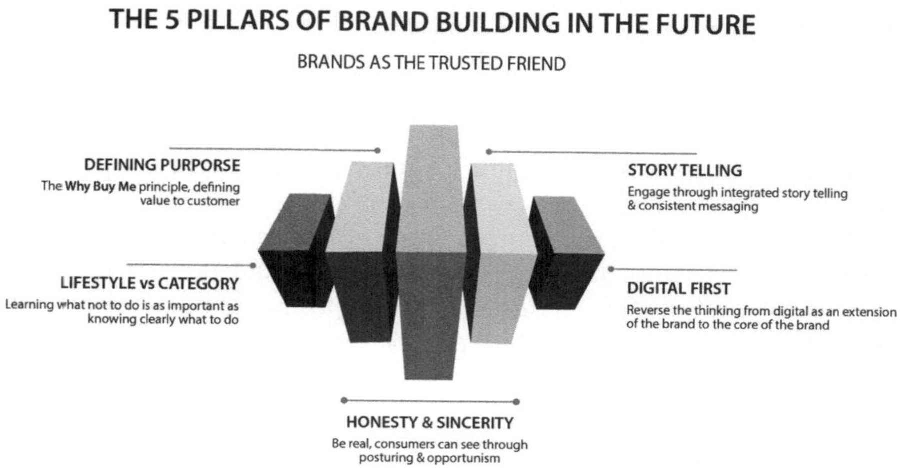

## Defining Purpose

This clearly states establishing - why does a brand need to exist and what is it doing for the consumer.

This is what I call the '**Why buy me Principle**' for e.g., in the Indian domestic market, we have a plethora of mass-value fashion brands/retailers (not taking names, referring to all of them without any exception) but what exactly is their purpose except that 'we sell cheap clothes/fashion'.

Whereas, when seen in the international context - a Uniqlo, Zara, H&M have clearly defined what they mean to the consumer. Their positioning is very clear - unique value-added products at low prices, quick adoption of fashion from ramp to the masses and mass production of trendy fashion.

To be relevant in the long run, grow exponentially and leave a clear niche in the consumer psyche, brands need to clearly differentiate and position themselves. This is even more relevant in today's noisy landscape.

Now, let's move to another very interesting facet of the fashion brands - the **obsession with becoming lifestyle brands**.

## Lifestyle vs. Category

Brands no more dictate lifestyle choices as consumers absorb them from different social media sources. Influencers are a '**thing**' today, peddling lifestyles to all. Rarely do we come across someone who buys a complete ensemble of a mannequin or for instance, picks up everything from the same store for decorating the home. Mostly, everyone mixes and matches.

While brands offer a complete lifestyle to establish a 'lifestyle approach', their sales mix is usually dominated by one category. Some of the most iconic brands are category-based/predominant brands for e.g., Levis.

With online shopping becoming a more dominant sales channel, the consumer is usually exposed to only a category and not the complete offering. So, the question I pose is: Should brands not put in energy, effort and resources in the same proportion in categories as the sales that it begets?

A simple fix to managing this is knowing when to switch from category to lifestyle. Many brands have bitten the dust by spending disproportionate amounts in building retail and lifestyle offerings when they may have done extremely well if they were category-focused.

Businesses should take clear positions on categories in some channels, while reducing the lifestyle offerings to only owned or controlled spaces. Wouldn't this help improve inventory productivity? Even today, brands offer nonmoving categories to complete the offering. Does anyone look at the cost of carrying inventory in the name of offering a complete mix, particularly when the consumer is clearly not buying?

There is nothing wrong with Lifestyle Brands, but sometimes a category-based play may well be a smarter one. This choice should be a well calibrated one, otherwise this may be a one-way trip to an early exit.

**Learning what not to do is as important to brand building as knowing what to do.**

But defining 'why and where to play alone' is not sufficient. Let's discuss how brands can stay relevant in this new reality.

## Story Telling

Indian fashion brands tend to be opportunistic in their communication. Now, whether it is because of the frequent churn at the top, sheer opportunism, bottom line pressures or a typical Indian disregard for our own history, or a combination of all these, I do not know.

But it's important to tell stories. They are engaging and they help build relationships and values with the consumer. But to tell stories, brands need to know themselves. They need to build a shared purpose and history with the consumer. They need to celebrate wins and take social positions based on their own positioning.

This story telling needs to be **consistent**.

That way the customer feels that he knows you, there is familiarity. A classic case of consistency in India is possibly – Max - you know exactly what you will get in their stores. Internationally, it could be Nike. Frequent reinventing the brand can alienate the consumers, therefore changes must be handled subtly.

But let's not divert from the topic. The questions are:

- Do our brands archive? Do they catalogue their history? What was the 1st garment they sold? Which is their best-selling SKU? Do they have a museum/library of their archives? Do they take pride in their history and values?
- Are they sharing inside stories of victories and struggles with their consumers?
- Do they control their narrative themselves?
- Most importantly, is it integrated across all media, retail, online etc.?

In this new reality, brands need to start becoming virtual people, confidantes, a friend to the consumer. Brands that do that will find it easy to build loyalty even in this world of transitory relationships.

Story telling is not very expensive, but it takes dogged persistence and in today's digital environment, it makes for compelling engagement.

But is that enough? How do we then win consumers' trust?

## Honesty and Sincerity

Consumers have become cynical with opportunism and posturing from brands. The number of scams and exposés in the recent past have taken the sheen away from businesses. The trust factor is gone.

A classic example would be 'greenwashing'. Several brands in the recent past have been taken to task for misleading consumers and making them feel good about their purchases.

How do you build Honesty and Sincerity?

There is no easy way out here. It must be through clearly laid down values which are demonstrated by senior management and communicated through all consumer touch points. Need I repeat that integrated and consistent approach to this is the only way. A classic example here would be the Tata brand.

So, it's not true that brands cannot influence consumers like they used to. The truth is that they need to build credibility, something that takes time along with consistency and an integrated approach to building brands. Consumers can see through you, and in a world where no secret can be hidden for long, only genuine values will win in the long run.

And finally, let's talk about accepting and facing reality.

## Digital First Brands

Brands need to reconfigure their businesses into becoming digital first. What does this phrase even mean today? Is this just a jargon? Let's understand in simple words.

- Do we manage our websites as flagship stores?
- What percentage of our online sales come from our own website?
- Do we review online sales with the same intensity as we do our retail sales?
- Are our fulfilment centres geared for e-commerce?
- Do we manage our own digital marketing?
- Have we created the right set of competencies in the brand?
- Are we planning merchandise and supply chains differently for online businesses?

Building sales through online channel partners by managing them like key accounts is not thinking digital. Most brands, today, look at online as another channel. They still think brick & mortar and go digital by extension. The trick is in reversing this thinking.

## To Conclude

I would simply say that most brands are still living in their glory days. They need to evolve into becoming a trusted friend, who is consistent and engaging in a virtual world: they need to become virtual companions.

Month-end pressures and living quarter-to-quarter is a reality. But to not build the brand while still managing operational issues is condemning the business to an eternity in duress.

Today, it is still possible to grow through physical expansion as the economy is still opening. But in the very near future, as the markets mature, these questions will come back to bite us. This will happen as the consumer gets more discerning with social media and international brands keep upgrading them.

Building the brand will define who survives and grows in the future.

CHAPTER 1.3

# The Future of Fashion Design

This is the third article in the '**Future**' series that explores the changing landscape of the fashion industry and the evolution of various functions & stakeholders in it. In this article, I have discussed the evolving role of fashion design.

In this article, '**design**' refers to commercial fashion design for brand/retail and not couture.

To begin with, we will first discuss:

- Recommendation on brand categorisation and its use in creating effective and relevant design team structure
- How to build competencies based on product strategy
- Go beyond the concept of seasons
- Move to managing multiple calendars
- Evolve to a digital-first world
- To conclude, I will also talk about how this impacts the day-to-day life of a designer

Before moving ahead we should revisit how I have defined the words '**Fashion**' and '**Trend**' differently here, but for quick reference 'fashion' refers to the brands' ability to dictate what to wear and 'trends' is about evolving consumer taste which gains mass appeal.

I work on a very simple categorisation of brands:

## How To Categorise Brands for This New Emerging Market?

As we saw in the previous article, brands no longer impact or set trends the way they used to in the 80's, 90's and the early 2000's. So, based on this, I have redefined how we could classify brands. Simply put, there are three variants:

**Trend Makers** - Consumers look up to these brands for setting new trends/fashion.

**Trend Experimenters** - Brands that constantly experiment with new trends and bring them to the larger consumer base.

**Trend Adopters** - Brands that replicate and mass manufacture the trends, making it available to one and all.

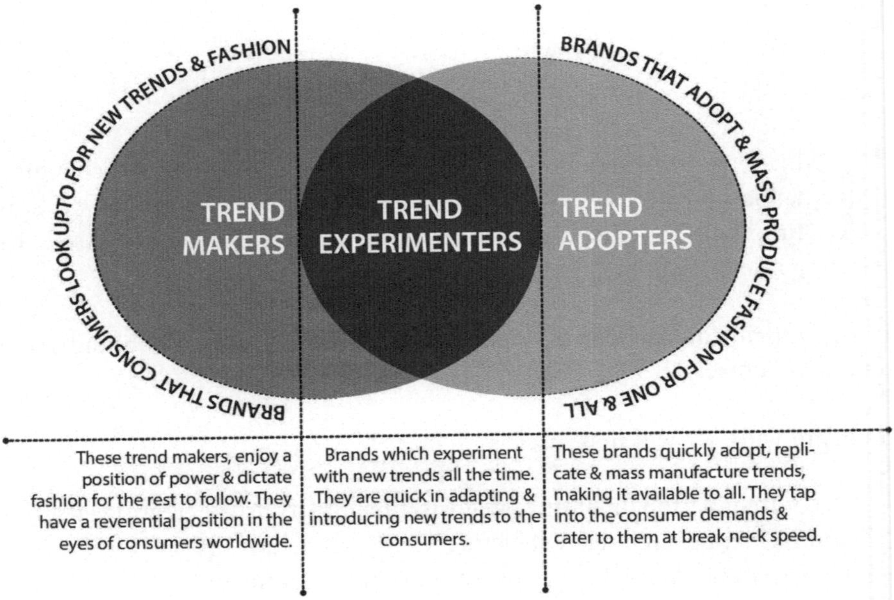


**Note - This categorisation is based on inferences drawn from personal experience. At the time of publication, I have not come across other authors who have used this scheme to categorise brands. If you, the reader, have come across such a source, do share it in the comments below.*

Having defined the business segment, we now move on to how we should structure our design teams to get the best value for the business.

## Structure Design Teams Differently to Manage Different Business Segments

I have always maintained that design teams should be structured differently for different business models. What works for a trend maker will not work for a trend adopter following trends.

A properly structured team can be of immense value to business. So, to attach designers to some buying teams, in a scattered manner - as is the case in many companies - may also not be a desirable solution.

The role of design should change from forecasting to innovation to trendspotting, based on the category of brand. However, there is something of these elements in each category of brands, just in varying degrees, based on how their brand is positioned as given in the infographic below.

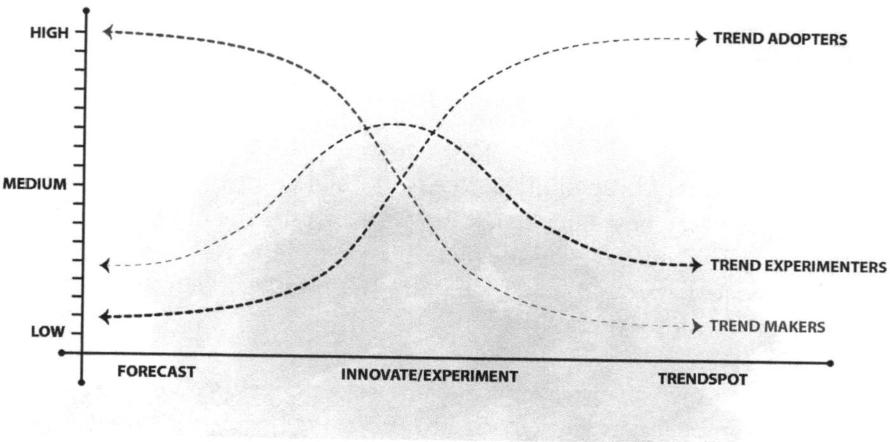


In India, the role of the design teams and how they should be structured, is not well understood. I cannot stress enough, how properly structuring a design team can greatly enhance reaction time and speed to market, thus enhancing business value many times over.

Here are two important aspects I want to point out:

1. In brands, where trend-spotting and quick response is important, I always feel that it is better to have two verticals within the design team
   (a) **The classical design team**, that forecasts fashion, manages brand salience, gives direction and creates designs and
   (b) **Curates and manages co-create** with other partners to ensure quick response to market.
2. Brands need to structure design teams in a way that works best for them. But across the world today, design teams are being moved to a more disaggregated way of working. Many, category-specialist, design teams are being relocated to factories. In some cases, vendors are being asked to set up design teams to support the brands. This allows for flexibility and faster speed to market.

Now let's understand product strategy and how to build capabilities around it for effectiveness.

## Build Design & Innovation Capabilities Based on Product Strategy

Typically design and innovation capabilities should be built based on the following principle:

- **Dominate** - What we are known for
- **Excel** - What we are good at
- **Manage** - Where we are present

And the way to build capability is to ensure total control on the 'Dominate Category' - get the best talent, support with investment in innovation and market it well. Then have an adequate play between create and curate for the 'Excel Category'. And finally, handle the 'Manage Category' through collaboration with partners.

Brands should own the direction and the selection of products going into their lines - but is it necessary to create everything by oneself?

Having large design teams slows down the reaction time to market and obsessing over originality can prove very expensive in terms of time lost, particularly when one can be original through smart curation.

## Move From Season to Go-To-Market Cycles

The myth of seasonal planning and launches has been bust. Seasons used to be about getting the consumer to refresh their wardrobes ensuring higher buys. Now, the consumer has moved to buying whenever they want. With promotions going round the year, brands need to plan their go-to-market cycles more frequently and design teams need to align to this.

The challenge here is to maintain the homogeneity and look & feel of the brand along with multiple drops, curation and ensure that the consumer feels at home even with such frequent launch cycles.

## Have Different Calendars for Different Categories and Channels

Go-to-market cycles can and should be different for different categories based on their lead times, and for various channels based on their requirements to re-fresh. Which would then mean a different calendar, say for jeans, as against one for, say graphic tees and so on.

This means splitting the product line into multiple calendars with different go-to-market deadlines and cycles. This can exponentially increase response time to market, if managed with rigour.

And now, let's talk about the most fundamental change taking place in design.

## Design Is Moving into the 3rd Dimension

3D is the defining change in the tech side on design. This will ease visualisation by internal teams and customers, virtualising the sampling, fit testing and speeding up the complete process of concept-to-shelf.

Virtual roadshows, testing design on controlled social media and allowing selection through voting will not only reduce development cycles, but will also be the single most powerful tool in reducing sampling spends and enabling speed to market.

## Conclusion

Let me summarise the above-mentioned points from a 30k-height perspective and what it would mean for the designers in day-to-day working.

1. **Research has a new meaning**. Designers must expand their horizons beyond forecasting agencies. They must look at unconventional resources like social media, streaming platforms, politics, sports as everything ignites a trend these days.
2. **Aquire new skill sets.** Integrate within their work style 3D softwares, virtual draping softwares, virtual fittings on 3D models, virtual fashion shows, virtual roadshows, online visual merchandising to name a few.
3. **Change in team structuring.** One person cannot do it all. Apart from creators and curators, specialists in 3D softwares may also be needed.
4. **Change in processes and prioritisation.** Relook at how tech packs are created? Do we have the time to follow conventional methods? With virtual coming to the forefront, hand and feel may lose priority. What one sees is what sells. Designers need to keep this in mind. With consumers also shifting to online buying, the optics of the product have higher relevance.
5. **Commercial calls.** We no longer have the time to obsess over smaller details. The bigger picture must be given more importance. A 'not so right' product at the 'right time' will make more money than a 'perfect product' at the 'wrong time'. Once the trend is obsolete, the merchandise is wasted. It does not matter if it matches the Pantone perfectly.

6. **Work on smaller, closer to market ranges and manage multiple calendars** instead of working on one big seasonal launch. Create & curate small collections which tie into larger stories.
7. **Behavioural changes required.** Start managing relationships with vendors. Become educators who can guide vendors in understanding the brand handwriting and ethos. Designers need to think out of the box, not just in design but also in processes.

CHAPTER 1.4

# The Future of Fashion Buying

This is the **fourth article** of the '**Future**' series exploring the changing world of the fashion industry and what it means for its various stakeholders. In this chapter, I shall be discussing the evolving role of the **Buying and Merchandising** function in the Brands and Retail companies.

To keep it simple, for this article, the term '**Buying**' refers to the buying, merchandising, product management and planning functions. The term '**Brands**' refers to both fashion and retail brands.

Many important topics like - the changing relevance of seasons, product strategy, fashion vs. trends, multiple go-to-market calendars, have already been covered in the previous article, hence I am not touching upon it again.

But, before we start, let's look at why this central function needs an overhaul? As we discussed in the first article, fashion brands are no longer in the driver's seat, they don't dictate trends anymore. So, brands find it increasingly difficult to forecast sales accurately in these uncertain times which leads to:

- Inefficient inventory buildup and reduced availability of right merchandise
- Lower sales, higher inventories and higher markdowns

So, In this Article, I Will Talk About:

- Moving to inventory planning linked to sales
- Building a bestseller-led strategy through 'test and repeat' merchandising
- The importance of defining the product architecture by supply chain logic
- Supported by a segmented approach to OTB management
- Augmented by dynamic pricing
- Finally, the use of AI to, improve inventory efficiency and increase profitability for brands in the future.

Hence, let us explore how businesses can be more robust and closer to their consumers, starting with removing an anomaly in the thinking that drives planning today.

## Move From 'Inventory Made for Planogram' To 'Sale-Based Inventory'

Planograms are the holy grail of retail. There are numerous AI-driven softwares that help visualise and manage this complex architecture. Unfortunately, brands use a cluster of different planograms to plan storage and display in different types of stores, and then use that capacity for filling the store with inventory.

Planograms should be viewed more as display optimiser to enable higher sales through better visibility rather than an inventory tool. Modern store fixtures are flexible and allow for open or stacked displays enabling reducing or increasing inventory holding capacity.

Hence, inventories must be reflective of sales and not planned for filling up fixed planograms. Once the inventory is defined (ideally based on weeks cover), then planograms should be used to optimise visibility.

I have often found this to be an extremely misunderstood concept amongst buying and planning teams, which keep filling up inventory in stores without it having a direct link to sales.

Having understood that the first step is to buy what can be sold as against to buying to fill display areas or complete the offering, we now move to discussing more fundamental changes in the operations of the Buying and Planning function.

## Building A Bestseller-Led Strategy

This is probably the only industry where goods come in with a deliberately, limited shelf life as we have pre-decided the products' fate. Imagine if car models had to be taken out every six months to pave the way for new cars, what would happen to their inventory and markdowns?

However, the question I ask is - Is this pre-defined life cycle relevant anymore?

Brands define their product line based on their understanding of their own positioning and what they perceive the consumer will buy from them.

But in reality, post launch, the market clearly repositions a brand in terms of how they perceive it and what they want to buy from it. And we know this through their bestselling products.

This is what I refer to as the '**Bestseller strategy**' for brands. This means that every product that becomes a fast-moving bestseller should be immediately moved to a 'replenishment pipe' – with defined threshold ROS (rate of sale), below which it should be discontinued. This is the way all other industries operate – but why not fashion?

**<u>Bestsellers should meet three qualifying factors:</u>**

- It should be a high velocity product
- It should be possible to be put on a replenishment pipe
- It should have wide acceptability across channels and geographies

Of course, this needs a calibrated approach – for e.g., faddish products, long leads etc., cannot be taken on replenishment even if they become bestsellers – may be repeated, but not replenished.

Basically, do brands need to rethink core as well? Should their bestsellers become core, rather than piling up inventory, offering products which are 'classic by definition' as core, but no one is buying? These are questions which I would like the reader to consider and comment on.

But the question then becomes - How do brands consistently score hits or in other words bestsellers?

## Move To A 'Test and Repeat' Merchandising Strategy

Buying is as much an art as it is a science. Some of the best buyers are those who can smell a bestseller way in advance and take a punt on the numbers, thereby **maximising sales** and **profits**. But these legendary buyers are hard to come by.

Here, I must mention that there are many **AI-based tool**s that promise to rate or predict product saleability or identify trends. Well, this may help in guiding product creation, but the actual hits can only be assured with requisite testing.

So, how do companies keep scoring hits? Social networking provides an amazing opportunity as does sample testing in select channels.

**Here are a few tips:**

- Create a limited test group for testing new products, connected through social networking.
- Keep launching new products, styles in that group - get it rated, tested and based on that decide on what to proceed with.
- This creates fertile ground to keep innovating and experimenting with trends. It becomes even more viable if designs are presented in 3D where the customer can't make out that it is not a real sample, allowing for quick decision-making even before test ordering.

This is a simple solution to creating more hits through testing. The trick in quick go-to-market and product launch is in operating with platformed raw materials. This is today being used by most tech savvy brands – a simple way to keep scoring hits in the business.

But how do we build these strategies into our product architecture in a way that optimises supply chain?

## Building The Product Architecture Based on Supply Chain Pipes

The key to this is really marrying back-end supply chain with demand planning and buying. Let's first understand what the supply chain pipes (clustering supply logic through different rules and lead times) are. They can be simply explained as in this infographic:

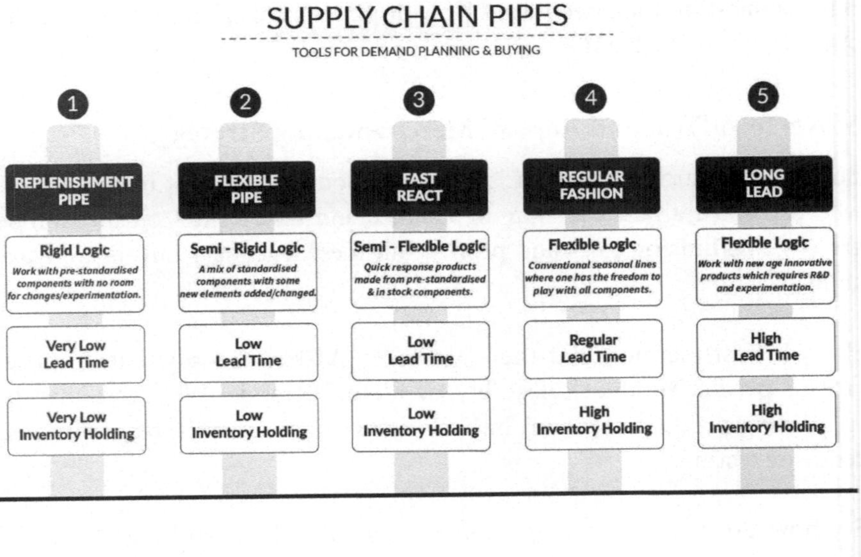

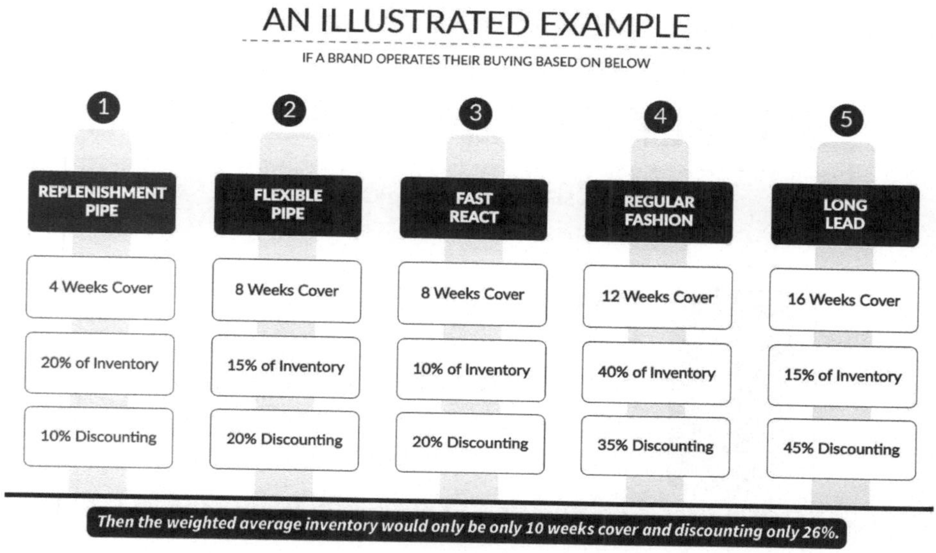


It's simplistic working and is very easy to understand. But why is this not followed by most companies?

Well, two reasons (a) because of multiple channels – operating with their own demand rules and (b) the product architecture is not made with this logic in mind.

The buying team holds the 'can' on this and getting design, supply chain, demand planning and sales teams to align all the external stakeholders to ensure that this works, is the key to becoming inventory and margin efficient in the future.

The product line architecture must be made with these pipes in mind, and different calendars and rules must be applied to product design, order trigger and go-to-market strategy to make this work.

But to try all this we need to have OTB, how does that get sorted?

## Segmented Approach to OTB Management

The most dreaded word for the buyer is OTB or Open-to-Buy. There never seems to be enough money available to buy what is truly needed. The best approach is to manage OTB for each supply chain segment differently, as explained in the infographic.

## SUPPLY CHAIN PIPES & OTB

A SEGMENTED APPROACH

**OPEN OTB PULL BASED**

**REPLENISHMENT PIPE**

Being pull based, should have an open OTB with clearly defined sales threshold & availability parameters.

**SEPARATE OTB**

**FLEXIBLE/ FAST REACT PIPE**

A semi pull/push based model, needs separate OTB, based on the number of Go-to-Market cycles, threshold inventory and sales.

**SEASONAL OTB**

**REGULAR/ LONG LEAD PIPE**

Needs to be managed through regular interval OTB, with some small value kept aside for in-season repeats or fresh fashion as the case may be.

The issue with managing 'buy' values is that mostly these segments are not managed separately. This leads to unjustified spends in each segment, and hence does not allow for 'buy optimisation'.

While this increases the buying inefficiency, how does one then reduce markdowns, keep inventory less and freshness high in the channels?

## Move To Dynamic Pricing

Or should I say dynamic markdowns. This means tracking products and their **ROS (Rate of Sale)** rigorously and marking down products basis how they are faring without waiting for end of season.

**This dynamic pricing model should:**

- Allow for different locations, colours, sizes to sell at different prices based on product performance.
- Be dynamic and the markdown should keep changing with time and ROS.
- Also sometimes incentivise future buys through coupons instead of just markdowns.

This will result in increased sales, less inventory during clearance and lower markdowns. This lower inventory, during clearance, will allow brands to sell fresh merchandise in the hopes of catching early bestseller trends and increasing trading weeks for fresh merchandise.

But is this level of detail humanly possible?

## The Use Of AI

Technology is changing the world and it should also be used to bring precision in the '**Buying Decision Making**' process. The best areas to use this are:

- Dynamic Pricing
- Predictive ROS (Rate of Sales)
- Bestseller Management aligned to Supply Chain Pipes
- Merchandise Financial Planning and OTB management aligned to Supply Chain Pipes
- 3D design for improved speed to market and testing

This use will free up the buying team's time and enable them to value add in other areas like innovation and promotions to name a few.

## Conclusion

We may all feel that this is all common sense. Well yes, but there are some legacy concepts in play, in the industry today, that needs to be challenged going forward. And that is what needs to change.

**<u>To recap:</u>**

1. Plan inventory linked to sales, not to display and offerings.
2. Stop looking at the business with a 'one size fits all' solution to calendars, product architecture, product launches, OTB management, markdowns and clearance sales.
3. Relook at product lifecycles – decision to take a product off should be based on rate of sales rather than some perceived period called 'season'. Imagine if best-selling car models were taken off shelves every six months just because the car company had to offer new line-ups every six months, what will the scenario be?

Treating each product on its own merit is the only solution to higher efficiency.

CHAPTER 1.5

# The Future of Fashion Sourcing

This is the **penultimate** post in the '**Future**' series - a set of 6 articles - that explores the changing face of the fashion industry. In this article, I will discuss how the sourcing function needs to undergo a change to keep fashion companies abreast of their new realities.

For this article, the term '**Sourcing**' refers to the procurement, manufacturing and quality functions in the fashion industry.

In this chapter, I will discuss how the sourcing function needs to:

- Redefine objectives and sourcing structures
- Relook at how we define costs
- Move to a 'consulting' from 'policing' way of working
- Go digital - and all that it entails to ensure that fashion companies are ahead of the curve

Let's start the discussion with understanding the purpose of having a sourcing function.

Is the function relevant anymore?

## Redefine Objectives and Sourcing Structures

Let us start with a little bit of history. The word **merchandiser** or merchant comes from the traders in the 1800's, who would come in their ships and display their wares to the buyers. And from there was also born this function called **sourcing**. Retailers would come to traders wanting them to source specific merchandise for their customers and stores.

In the golden age of fashion brands (80's through to the early 2000's), sourcing took on the role of ensuring lowest possible cost for products delivered on time and within defined quality parameters.

And this has been the legacy **'L1' (lowest cost)** sourcing.

As per capita incomes rose in manufacturing countries, sourcing organisations shifted to procuring from cheaper and cheaper locations like China, Bangladesh and now African countries. Unlike other industries, apparel retail prices have been very stable over the last few decades, in fact even coming down in many cases.

But is L1 a relevant objective in today's brave new world? A classic example would be Zara who is a value retailer but with high-cost procurement strategy. A sizeable amount of their production happens in Europe to enable faster speed to market.

Let's look at **Image - 01** to understand the four pillars of the sourcing function.

*Original infographic created by insideapparel.net

Fashion companies need to structure their sourcing teams and clearly define their KPI's based on their own business models, which we discussed in our previous article. Now, look at the importance of each of these four pillars. The way teams are structured will change to adapt to the brand positioning.

Image - 02

KEY DELIVERABLES & BRAND SEGMENTATION

WHAT THE SOURCING FUNCTION NEEDS TO FOCUS ON BASED ON BRAND SEGMENTATION APPROACH

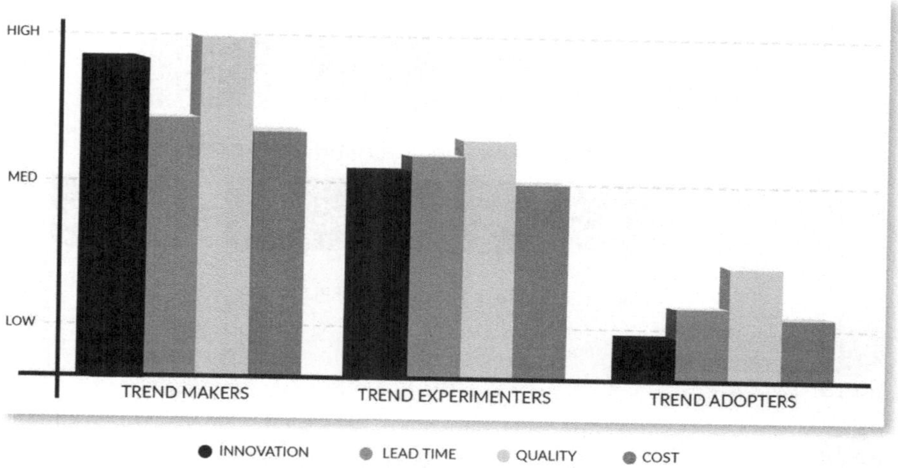


*Original infographic created by insideapparel.net

The above **Image – 02** is indicative and will differ case to case, but the working, key deliverables and structure of sourcing teams will depend on these varied requirements. All companies need these structures but in varying degrees, and that will determine the no. of people in each department, their strength and the processes they follow.

This brings us to another key aspect of the business - how do we define cost itself?

## Redefine How We Measure Cost

Today, the biggest issue with companies is the way they look at the product cost. The moment we shift from defining deliverables in terms of 'landed cost' to '**EPLC - end of product lifecycle cost**', the whole game changes. It is explained with a simplistic example in **Image - 03** below.

Image - 03

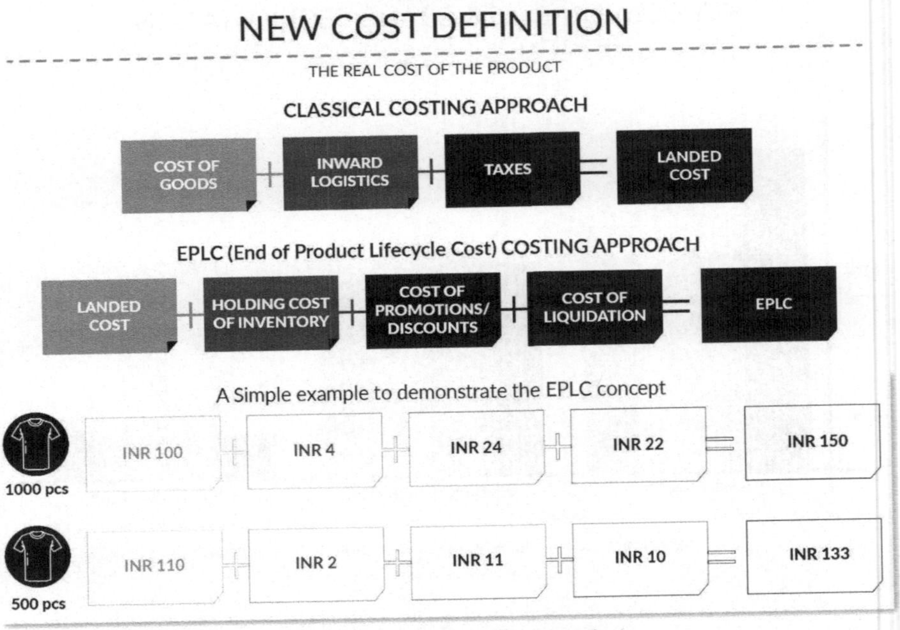


*Original infographic created by insideapparel.net

In the above example, while it appears that the product is more expensive at Rs 110, it is actually cheaper for the company. And this is where the real problem lies with pushing L1 costs across different supply chain pipes.

What is needed is a wholistic approach to cost (defined here as **EPLC**) and that is an organisational objective as against simple 'landed cost' which is a sourcing objective. Now, the moment an organisation starts mapping and reducing its EPLC, the following questions would need to be answered:

- Location of sourcing hub, near-shoring and speed to market
- Volume of purchase or buying small lots and multiple times based on demand
- Vendor as a curator/fashion innovator or as only a low-cost manufacturer

This will re-orient sourcing teams to think differently for the company.

But having understood that sourcing functions must move away from L1 sourcing to applying different sourcing models for different business requirements and different supply chain pipes. We need to now move to another topic, changing the very way in which we work.

## Move To Consulting from Policing

Currently sourcing and quality teams have a policing approach to the procurement and manufacturing function. The greater the control, the happier the sourcing teams.

## Where is trust? What happened to collaboration?

**<u>But the question I ask is more fundamental</u>:**

- In this new world, can companies continue to invest in very large sourcing and quality teams?
- Isn't quality and timely delivery the responsibility of the vendor? Then why do we need such large sourcing teams?
- How much of the work done by the teams is value adding to the company and what part is simply 'passing the parcel', 'follow up' and 'filling up data sheets?' Do we even need people for this work?

In the future, sourcing functions need to move to working in a manner where they are like a consulting function.

- Support vendors with becoming flexible and cost efficient
- Help brands and businesses with innovation, design, and development
- Negotiations, product re-engineering, source substitutions, strategic alignments for raw materials
- Train vendors to become better at managing their own quality

In the next section, we will discuss how digitisation will completely change the way sourcing organisations will function.

## Going Digital

The **Image - 04** speaks a thousand words. It gives a quick glimpse of how companies will work digitally in the future.

Image - 04

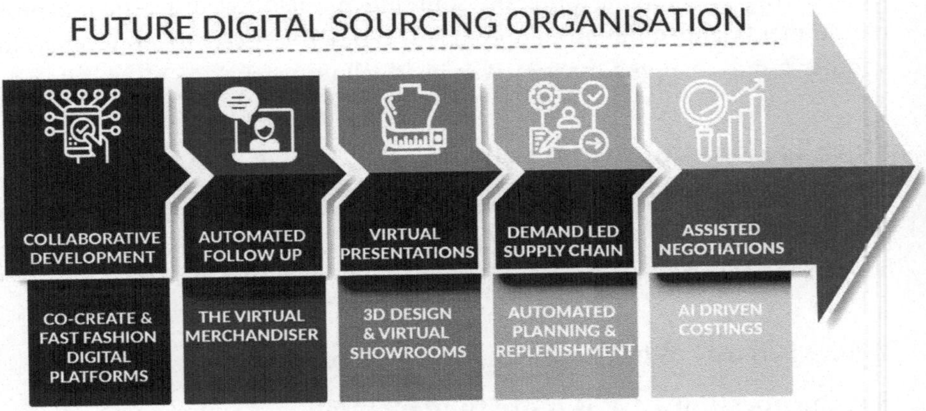


*Original infographic created by insideapparel.net

Apparel Supply Chains of the future will need to work with AI, virtual products and digital connectivity in ways that we have only begun to scratch the surface of. The real winners are going to be those who recognise this new oncoming reality and experiment with newer ways of working today, which will prepare them for tomorrow's reality. I am sharing some ideas of what the future may contain (and it is not too far away).

## Integrating Disintegrated Supply Chains Through Unified Virtual Marketplaces

With the digital platforms coming into the mainstream, disaggregated components of supply chain will be integrated into a single marketplace. Data will be available at a click of a button to all. This ease of access will lead to an integrated view of inventory, capacities, capabilities, prices, lead times and demand, enabling a seamless supply chain.

## The Virtual Merchandiser

A large part of the sourcing merchant's day is spent on mundane activities like follow ups and documentation. A virtual merchandiser will probably be an AI-based software that handles all these activities. In the future, this digital merchandiser may even be smart enough to take some of the decisions itself. Such applications may soon become the main stay in the sourcing function.

## Virtual Sampling, Process Enablement

World over, 3D softwares are replacing the conventional process of sketching, sampling and sample presentations. Today, the roadshows are just a click away. Virtual roadshows, digital or video approvals on design and fits are reducing months from the calendar and making business faster and agile.

## Demand Led Supply Chain

The '**Test & Repeat**' model is going to be the future of the apparel industry. Brands and retailers will make less or opt for virtual products to test. Only the products that work will be manufactured. Quick repeat orders will soon become a reality. Preparing for smaller lots with multiple quick replenishments will come into play.

## Digital Platforms, Managing Planning, Sourcing, Quality & Compliance While Connecting All Stakeholders

Future ready technology is enabling all business stakeholders to collaborate on digital platforms. This is shrinking the lead times and enabling everyone to make quicker decisions. This is also presenting a single source of truth in the whole supply chain, which will virtually eliminate hours of agonising and hundreds of man-days.

A single click platform is the future of the apparel industry and adoption of technology-based assistance is the way ahead for sourcing teams across the industry.

## Conclusion

The sourcing function needs to rediscover its purpose and value addition in this emerging new world. Today, a lot of fashion companies suffer from this preconceived notion of how sourcing needs to function and what it is supposed to deliver. A hard look is required at some of our most dearly held ideas.

**To quickly summarise, I would simply say:**

- **Digital** is the only way forward. The pandemic has really brought this to light and probably started the process of fast-forwarding adoption

- Sourcing needs to rediscover its purpose, **restructure and realign** itself to be relevant in today's changing market
- Fashion companies need to **relook** at some of their cherished ideas about L1 sourcing and how to measure costs

CHAPTER 1.6

# The Future of Fashion Vendor

This is the final article in the '**Future**' series - a set of 6 articles - on the changing landscape of the fashion industry and what it means for its various stakeholders. We started this series with changing consumer trends and in this article, we will understand how it impacts the supplier base.

For this article, the word '**Vendor**' refers to finished goods, raw materials, trims and other ancillaries, which support the product manufacturing process. The term '**Brands**' shall refer to both fashion and retail companies.

Some relevant topics - like seasons, multiple go-to-market strategies, supply chain pipes, EPLC, digitisation of the disaggregated supply chain have already been covered in previous articles.

In this article, I will discuss how vendors need to:

- Position themselves to their customers
- Structure for flexibility
- Plan for additional financing
- Become fashion consultants and
- Digitise their operations to remain ahead in this quickly changing world.

So, let's start this discussion by quickly understanding how the brand requirements are changing and from that derive, what a vendor's strategy should be.

## Changing Brand Requirements

There are a few things changing in the fashion world. Brands are looking for the following and are willing to pay a premium for the same:

- Vendors handling smaller volumes with ease
- Vendors taking on some of the brand's inventory pressures
- Vendors bringing flexible working on the table in terms of delivery phasing, inventory parking to name a few
- Vendors who are also their trend, innovation, and design partners

The reasons for the above have been discussed in greater details in the previous chapters.

Having understood the above, let us first see how vendors should strategise to be relevant in the coming era.

## Vendor Positioning

I have a very simple way of looking at this that's explained in image no.1 below:

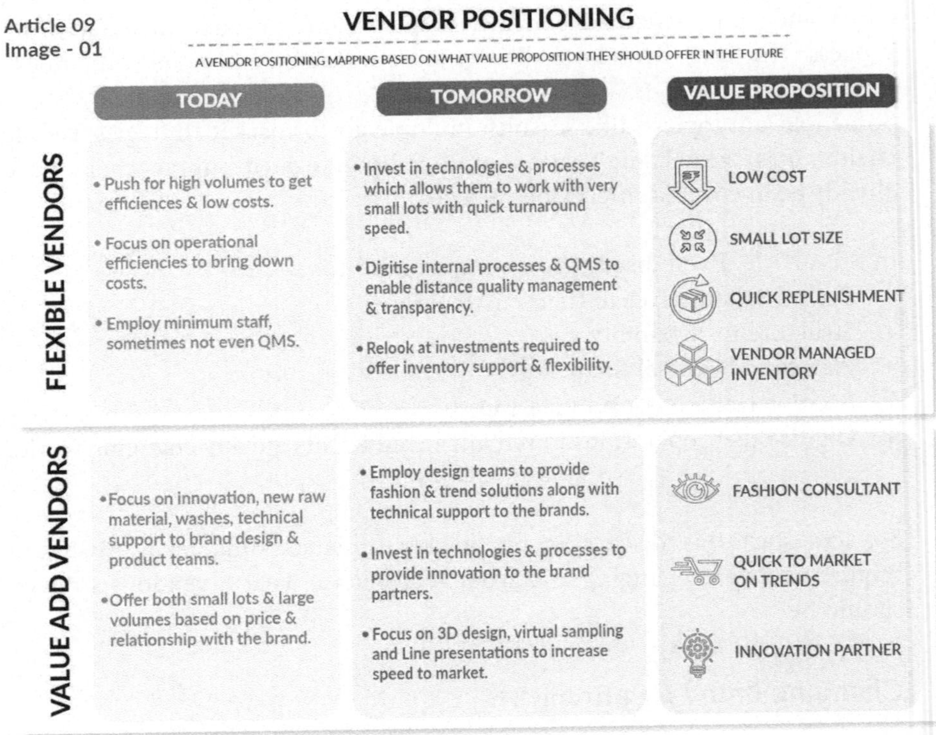


*Original infographic created by insideapparel.net

There are two other positions available as well **(a) the classic low-cost/high-volume vendor and (b) the niche vendor**. The low-cost/high-vol vendor will continue to face growth and uncertainty issues unless they transition to either flexible or value-add vendors.

This takes us to the next point, which is **flexibility**.

## Structure for Flexibility

Vendors like to have orders in hand (sometimes a full season's orders at a go, helping them fill their order books and planning lines well in advance) to manage their lines well, but brands are no longer able to forecast as before. Hence, they are looking at various ways like replenishment, vendor managed inventory and quick turnaround to manage their demand.

Brands want to drive demand-based supply, which is closer to market, that gives very little time for planning. However, vendors find this uncertainty difficult to manage.

Factories are built for volume, efficiency and cost reduction; this needs to move to flexibility with lot of sizes, digital solutions for flexibility and cost optimisation with an understanding of additional services being offered.

To set everyone's mind at rest, I should mention here that while there will be smaller lots, it does not mean overall volumes will decline. It is just that it will be split into smaller lots. Vendors need to look at how their factories and procurement are organised to meet this. Can they manage quick changes, smaller lots without impacting their overall efficiency?

Stemming from this, let's discuss the next point - what is the meaning of '**managing some of the brand's inventory pressures**'?

## Vendor Managed Inventory

In an uncertain market, brands will need to look at different supply chain pipes. These pipes will be supported through platforming of inventory at various stages of the manufacturing process to enable **flexibility and speed to market**.

Earlier factories used to only look at costs and capacity bookings. They now need to work with their brand partners on inventory management, sales-based replenishment and quick-to-market launches for them.

This brings us to the next point which is **money**.

## Plan For Investments to Secure the Future

It's an often-repeated question, 'how are we to invest in all these, it will cost a lot of money'? Yes. But if the vendor clearly positions him/herself as one of the above then the business relationship will become a partnership rather than a contractual one. This will become an umbilical cord that cannot be quickly cut.

Vendors need to develop a sense of these requirements, which a brand has, and offer workable solutions rather than going to them with a manufacturing set-up with capacity and cost offerings.

This begs another question, why do vendors need to invest in **design**?

## Becoming Fashion Consultants

It's important that vendors start offering fashion, **trend, and innovation solutions** rather than products and technology. Brands need quick solutions in a fast-changing world. Doing everything by oneself takes time.

Vendors, managing design and development, can ensure **quicker go-to-market** solutions. This will increase business both for the brand and the vendor, alongside establish an unshakable position for the vendor.

Being a simple low-cost vendor is a commodity which will no longer yield benefits. Brands need solutions - this is where vendors need to pitch.

All this is a big ask. Flexibility means 'uncertainty' for the vendor. Can they handle so much uncertainty in their business? The answer lies in going digital.

## Digitise Operations

Factories still operate with analog systems. Even today, there are questions around digitisation. So, where should factories digitise and why? There are many good factory erp systems available, but factories need to gain scale to be able to afford them. But they must go beyond basic ERP systems to look at some cutting edge softwares. Some of these are given below:

- AI-based planning optimisation to manage quick changeovers, smaller lots, optimisation of workstations, material handling and integration of departments, allocation and optimisation of cost
- Payroll, upgradation, and skill management of workers
- 3D design for quick approvals, virtual sampling, and speed to market
- Automation of routine tasks like procurement optimisation, RFQ's, PO's - coordination of procurement and follow up for raw materials
- Digitise quality-management systems and compliance data management

And finally, providing a dashboard to their customers with live data on status, performance, and quality management of styles to build trust and transparency with the customer.

The above can seriously bring in maximum control, lower costs, higher efficiencies, and all data available on the click of a button.

## Conclusion

In India, vendor bases are small and scaling up is an issue. Labour, regulations, higher cost of capital and rising costs (subject for a future chapter) have laid waste to fertile business opportunities. On the other hand, brands are getting more and more organised, demanding transparency, dependability, consistency, and flexibility.

Can apparel manufacturers survive in this unfriendly environment? This is a question often asked by factories and vendors. Younger generations are not interested in continuing the family business, they feel the return on effort (ROE) is too low.

Caught up in this quagmire, how do vendors grow businesses?

To conclude, I would only say suppliers need to clearly redefine their objective and how they look at themselves. Move from being a provider of products to a provider of solutions and services. They must:

- Position their business clearly with their customer to stay relevant
- Build long term associations through becoming a solution -provider rather than a manufacturer and,
- Digitise to overcome the uncertainty and challenges thrown up by the system and new market changes.

In the long run, vendors who look at adding value to their customers, either through clever supply chain solutions or design and innovations, will continue to grow even in these uncertain times, where their customers are trying to come to grips with the market.

CHAPTER 1.7

# From the Readers' Mind!

We, at Inside Apparel, had an exciting three months since our launch. This last series had a lot of feedback in the industry and has been a topic of many a discussion. Here, we are sharing some of the thoughts shared by our readers.

We've had so much and such diverse discussions from industry leaders, business owners and many senior colleagues, in our comments' section that it would have taken a book to write it all down so we would ask our readers to go through them sometime, at leisure.

We have been very lucky and privileged to have such a consistent readership and would request everyone to partake in their wisdom. We've not covered a few extremely detailed and thought-provoking comments here, but they will be featured as future articles. Enjoy.

## THE FUTURE IS IN EXECUTION

*"You are absolutely right that* ***while consumption patterns may not change, execution models will.*** *Companies need to move rapidly to relook at the cost models. Several core processes may have to be executed through a combination of in-house and outsourcing".*

- Krishna Kumar (KK) IT Entrepreneur and Supply Chain Enthusiast

## BRAND POSITIONING

*"I think that a herd mentality has taken over the Indian fashion brands where they try to outdo each other with massive discounts and offers, damaging the very foundations of the brand.* ***We seem to have forgotten the basic lessons of marketing: segment, position, differentiate and build a relationship with***

***your core customer to dominate the segment.*** *Most brands have confused targeting and positioning with unclear value proposition.*

*We don't need to look at international fashion brands for inspiration. Just look at the new wave of domestic brands like Man company, Bombay Shaving Co, etc. in personal care category. They seem to be following each of your recommendations to a fault. The Indian fashion brands have to ask a serious question- how much are they investing in Brand building vs how much they are frittering away in terms of discounts/offers?"*

- Krishna Kumar (KK) IT Entrepreneur and Supply Chain Enthusiast

## CATEGORY VS. LIFESTYLE

*"Category vs. Lifestyle is a classic struggle. We noticed that almost 80% of our sales were coming only in 2 categories. Yet we had a large inventory of other categories as we wanted to give the customer the full range. But as pressures of inventory came in, we slowly defaulted to being a category-focused brand. But what should large format retailers do? They need to carry everything".*

- Gunish Jain, CEO BlueKaktus

## THE IMPORTANCE OF INNOVATION

*"Just a thought,* ***Breakthrough product innovation helps reinventing the brands****, like Boost from Adidas, Airism from Uniqlo".*

- Ramesh Ramalingam, VP Sourcing Operations, Arvind Fashions

## STICK TO YOUR CORE

*"Sticking to one's core is important, I recollect even Gap moving away from their khaki chino, denim shirt and gap logo sweatshirt look in late 90's, getting their learnings and sticking to what they stand for. When we started our career in fashion industry 3 decades ago it was* ***"brand made a man" (or woman) and now the consumer defines, and brands adapt".***

- Kamal Gupta, Entrepreneur

## THE VIRTUAL DESIGNER

*"For designers-retail/clothing/fashion, it is now very important to be a virtual designer in every sense. Virtual being the keyword here. My little experience with entrepreneurship has totally reinforced this.* ***Traditional methods of working definitely need to be thrown out of the window and new design practices have to be adapted.*** *It's now or never as the customer in the coming*

*future is online. Virtual designing/ representation/ roadshows/ marketing need to be the strongest asset of any brand's design team - I can't stress more on that, or they will definitely die out".*

- Rupa Giani - Entrepreneur, Designer, Cofounder Qfamily, Cute and Cool

## DESIGNERS SHOULD HAVE A FREE HAND

*"I have a different outlook on this article and would like to use the platform to share it.*

*I think* ***designers should always have a free hand to try whatever they put them on, because the inception of an idea comes to life through their creativity.*** *Designers are storytellers, the world is their playground. They should be allowed to explore and create magic out of it. They are the ones who identify and connect with the mood of the world. Someone mentioned to me once - "Camo print came into fashion when the mood of the world was war". I honestly don't know if that was true, but it felt right, likewise even when the most glamorous looking women around the world, who wore bling at some point, switched their moods to becoming lazy & comfortable, we saw a paradigmatic shift to sneakers and sweatpants.*

***Expecting designers to understand the economics of the business may not be the right thing to do.*** *In my opinion, it would limit their creativity".*

- Neeraj Katoch, Sr. Mgr B&M, Arvind Fashions

## DESIGN WILL BE DRIVEN BY SALES

*"Gone are the days of ramp designs or formal suits. Let's study what's actually happening around us.* ***Design is going to be driven by sales as business scrambles to survive".***

- Poonam Sood Lal, Consultant, Co-Founder Sash Exports (Buying House)

## DESIGN IS RUDIMENTARY IN MOST COMPANIES

*"Designing digitally is the need of the hour. But somehow, I am not convinced at using a designer's creative time in doing clerical work as 3D rendering solves cataloging and physical roadshow problems especially in this COVID era, but it in no way solves a creative problem except better visualisation.*

*In my experience, India and the Indian brand & retail industry have a long way to go and learn how to use designers effectively. Designs are still being done in a very rudimentary manner in most of the companies.* ***I guess***

***we are yet to learn to look at design as a process and a problem-solving tool".***

- Rajesh Kumar, VP & Creative Director, US Polo Assn.

## DESIGN SCHOOLS SHOULD BE MORE INDUSTRY-ORIENTED

*"Perhaps fashion/design institutes should also connect with industry experts and understand how different businesses function and role of design in different business models.* ***It's time design internships and industrial training programmes with companies are structured in a meaningful and relevant manner by the fashion institutes.*** *This will help students and future design professionals understand the role of design which is beyond mood board, good aesthetics, colours and tech-packs".*

- Moutushi Dey, Design Consultant

## MANAGING DEMAND PLANNING IN CHANNELS TO OPTIMISE THROUGHPUT

*"In my view, there are several points that are important while discussing buying.*

- *Channels*
- *Sourcing lead times*
- *MOQ*
- *Flexibility of management*

*Channels: today brands are present in various channels.* ***Each channel expects different kinds of merchandise, sales price and margins.*** *If all the stores are owned by the brand, then many things can be controlled".*

- Prashanth HV, Product Strategy, Royal Enfield Apparel

## CENTRALISE INVENTORY TO REDUCE INVENTORY

*"Key to success would be to* ***consolidate inventory at inventory hubs*** *and make them visible to multiple stores. This would reduce multiple inventories holding points".*

- Himanshu Singh, Co-founder, Meraki

## AN INTERESTING ANECDOTE

*"This brings me to an interesting success story of my customer. This is a large French retailer with shops/stores across the globe. The designer herself was the buyer and sourcing person. She managed her product line (men's tee shirts). In,*

*so many years of sourcing for this customer, I never heard even once a word of high inventory, hence less buying.*

*Her style of working was incredibly unique. She would send the complete techpacks with her confirmed buying price and a tentative qty. She never wanted the samples. All she required was the yarn dips for colour approval. Once the yarn dips were approved, she would give a go ahead to start the process of production. Then she would ask us to produce about 1500 pieces per colourway and ship them to a few selected locations across the globe.*

*It is interesting to note that she would then come back to us within 10 days, whether to continue the production or drop the style. If continue, nothing wrong. She would get the delivery in her fixed delivery period. But the problem was if she asked us to stop the production. In such a case, she would then send the fresh style (using the same colours). Her take from this way of functioning were many folds.*

1. *She got to test the market.*
2. *If style did not move, the discounting was only on few hundred pieces and no blocked inventory.*
3. *She could always have freshness in the stores.*
4. *The vendor always remained loyal and was willing to experiment.*
5. *The product cost remained fixed.*
6. *Even a men's tee shirt category became a fast fashion instead of a boring product line.*

***To successfully merchandise a fashion retailer, whether it's a small boutique or major departmental store, it requires a proactive fashion representative, who is always up-to-date on the latest fashion trends, to understand what consumers want to buy".***

- Sanjay Lal, Co-founder, Sash Exports (Buying House)

## CREATING ARTIFICIAL SCARCITY AS A MERCHANDISE STRATEGY

*"This would require a complete overhaul of the structure of the buying and sourcing teams, and how they are incentivised. For example,* ***can buying be incentivised on ROS?*** *Also, how does a brand maintain its TRUE essence? For example,* ***is FRESHNESS a desired outcome?*** *Like Zara. Should retailers create artificial scarcity? Is that a good strategy?"*

- Gunish Jain, CEO, BlueKaktus

## DIGITISATION WILL INCREASE COSTS FOR THE VENDOR

*"While I fully subscribe to the digitisation in the Supply Chain and companies investing heavily into the software, it is left to be seen how the vendor will adopt the same. How the vendor will sync with the retailer. It is also true that every retailer will be careful of not exposing or sharing the data with vendors. On the other hand, there will be a risk of data theft, hacking, virus attacks from third party system, forcing the retailers to invest heavily in protection. This means the cost of the digitisation goes up for the vendor.*

*Retailer will be foolish to think that after passing the digitisation he will have a monopoly on the vendor. Sourcing knows vendor cannot survive on one customer and manufacturer for number of other retailers.* ***This translates that the vendor will need similar digitisation with other customers, resulting into the cost increase for the vendor. Is it financially viable for the vendor?"***

- Sanjay Lal, Co-founder, Sash Exports (Buying House)

## SHIFTING RESPONSIBILITIES AND OWNERSHIP BETWEEN STAKEHOLDERS

***"Your articles talk about the shifting of responsibilities and ownership between different roles and development of new skills while adopting technology at various levels.***

*Especially, if we read the last two, between sourcing and vendors, a lot of responsibilities which are currently resting with the sourcing teams will move 'actively' to the vendor, with the sourcing team mainly playing a consulting role.*

*However, the vendor wanting to adopt the changes and digitisation and technological advances - that will help him get there - he will need to invest more not only in setting the processes and technologies, but more importantly getting the right people do run them. Overall, this would mean cost increase for the vendor. However, with the vendor actively taking this role up, the sourcing offices would be able to cut back a lot of their costs. At an overall level, because it's shifting of responsibilities and getting rid of some amount of duplication and improvement of efficiency, it should lead to overall cost reduction/better margins which can both be divided between the vendor and the brand.*

***It would however be interesting to see how the costs will shift, as the cost at the vendor's end is bound to increase with this level of investment, but it should be more than nullified by the savings at the sourcing office's end".***

- Garima Joshi, Co-founder Meraki

## WHEN YOU HAVE INFORMATION, YOU NEED NOT CARRY INVENTORY

*"Highlighting the fast changes that the market is witnessing, Anindya has brought out the importance of change in mindset that is required across the supply chain.*

1. *Transparency between the various parties involved- I will blame both the vendor and the brand for holding their cards too close to their chests. High time you laid them bare*
2. *Trust – both parties need to work on these over long periods and interactions*
3. *Need for investment in new technologies and software*
4. *Need for adapting newer approaches to solving problems*

*3 and 4 will be futile without 1 and 2.* ***In the book 'World is Flat', the author says, 'when you have information you need not carry inventory'.*** *Something I have cherished reading".*

Ram Subramanium, MBA, PMP, Scrum Master, Principal Consultant at Global Channel Solutions Inc

## BRANDS MUST SUPPORT VENDORS IN DEVELOPING THEM TO HANDLE DESIGN

*"We do understand the market was already changing from past 2-3 years but now the responsibility is double for the vendor after covid 19. In fact, most of the vendor do not have sufficient people to handle the brands/design development or capacity to invest on new innovation .. in this case brands also need to come forward and share the investment on vendors as* ***we can see buyers are investing in Bangladesh/Vietnam and also guiding them for technology/designing.***

***Brands must visualise the strength of vendor/capacity and try to work with limited number of vendors so you can give maximum number of months load to them and get priority from vendor too".***

- RP Singh, President, Eveline International

## WHY ARE WE NOT CHANGING?

*"The fashion has to have speed to market, a lean production system, designers and 3D design technology with MIS systems built in. It is this fashion that will actually bring the customer to the factory, and the core will be a support system.*

*Why are we not looking at lean manufacturing?*

*Why are we not investing in 3d Design technology?*

*Why don't we have an inbuilt MIS system which can have a live production status on the cloud every morning for the customer to simply log in?*

***In today's world unless we evolve both at customer and factory level, we are going to find ourselves redundant and out of business".***

- Poonam Sood Lal, Consultant, Co-Founder, Sash Exports (Buying House)

## LABOUR LAWS NEED TO CHANGE

*"Among all the aspects discussed, I feel one of the important aspects* ***is, the existing labour situation from farm to frontend which is preventing people to think this industry as an option and do any sort of investments - be it expansion, upgradation etc....*** *If it becomes conducive, may attract more home-grown business houses and global players.*

*Labour engagement is one of the key factors. We need some holistic approach like,* ***can union govt. scheme MGNREGA get integrated with labour intense industries like us? It will incentive the workforce and entrepreneurs*** *and will also pave the way for global players to explore Greenfield investments.*

*And without a stable apparel supply chain ecosystem, with no choice, domestic apparel brands and retailers will be forced to look at overseas sources, but govt. policies may not encourage.*

*It is a catch 22 situation".*

- Ramesh Ramalingam, VP Sourcing Operations, Arvind Fashions

## THE NEED FOR A NEW GENERATION OF ENTREPRENEURS

*"Unfortunately garment manufacturing is one of the lowest tech industries. And the margins are low.* ***So, when the 1st generation built this and educated their children, the children preferred to venture into newer and advanced industries (tech, services etc.).***

*I feel for this industry to thrive in India, manufacturing has to shift to the hinterlands,* ***new 1st generation entrepreneurs, who have the hunger and desire to make garments should come up.***

*Also, vertical integration with the fabric supply chain is also the need of the hour. That is the only way economies of scale will be built and RMG vendors will have the size and scale to invest in technology".*

- Gunish Jain, CEO, BlueKaktus

## Conclusion

One thing is clear. Change is inevitable. While most readers agreed with the future of the fashion industry discussed in these chapters, there is a general feeling that indicates we are unprepared to move into the future.

Well, if we don't change, a new industry with new players will rise like the phoenix and then we will be trying to play catch up.

# PART 2

# THE MYTHS IN FASHION DESIGN

***We have busted some myths but there are many more to go!!***

Many believe that design is an art, and the designer, an artist. But the reality is far from that. Designing, to me, is a commercial art - one which has rather big implication. A designer's job is not to just create a beautiful design, but to create a design that sells and is accepted by a larger consumer base.

This part - '**The myths in fashion design**' - is written with the aim to shed light on what really happens in the fashion industry and bust a few accepted and unaccepted myths.

CHAPTER 2.1

# How Many Colours are Too Many?

This is a very interesting subject and one that I have been wanting to write on for a very long time. In this chapter, I will dwell upon the following:

1. The importance of colour
2. My three rules of colour
3. How many colours are too many colours
4. How ignoring these can impact business

Let us start this discussion by understanding,

## The Importance of Colour

"Did you know that **84.7%** of the consumers make a purchase decision based on colours?"

A google search revealed 32 pages of web links available on the subject; **Importance of Colours**. Colours don't just affect emotions, but drive consumer choices, their buying behaviour, brand recognition & much more.

Why is the UCB logo green? Adidas logo black? And Levi's logo red?

Are these colours randomly picked?

The answer is "NO".

And the below infographic tells you why…

There is enough and more research available, yet when we look at our domestic fashion brands, we get a feeling that they lack an understanding of the **Science of Colour**.

Often, we see, brands & retailers trying to appeal to all with a riot of colours. How often do we hear these phrases, 'let's add some more colours' or 'can we do 10 colours in this?'

### Why is there such recklessness in decision-making about colours?

Is it because the brands take decisions on colours without understanding that every colour decision is an investment decision?

Or is it because volumes are still not large in most brands, so taking risk on colours is financially not a big decision?

But I am getting ahead of the subject here. First, let us understand some simple rules in working with colours.

## The 1st Rule of Colour

The rule is '**Less is more**' when it comes to colours.

There can be 2 kinds of stores & brands: ones which are Directional (offering limited & unified colour range) & ones which are Multilateral (offering many colours).

Multiple studies reveal that a directional store holds the consumers' interest for longer as it appeals to their emotions and has a calming effect on them. And the more time they spend in the store, more likely they are to make a purchase.

## The 2nd Rule of Colour

The rule is '**Balance the proportion of dare to easy**' colours in the line.

When it comes to colours in clothes, there are 2 kinds: ones which are **easy to wear** and ones which **dare you to wear** them. It is very important to understand the proportion of dare and ease in colours, designs and silhouettes, which you offer to the consumers. So, the rule is simple - do not have more than one dare element per style and make sure that there are enough easy-to-wear products.

If we study the average consumers' wardrobe, we will find it to be dominated by easy-to-wear colours, with just a sprinkling of experimental colours, usually reserved for occasions.

Knowing what not to do is as important as knowing what to do. A simple 'what not to do' can vary from mixing unpalatable colours to making experimental (dare to wear) styling in 'dare to wear' colours. It's like a double dare.

## The 3rd Rule of Colour

The rule is '**Increase colour offering in key/signature fast moving products, keeping the rest directional**' to increase saleability and mitigate risk.

For many brands, colour is a strategy. The brand DNA is built around offering a plethora of colours. A classic example of this is United Colors of Benetton. But upon studying such brands, you will realise that a plethora of colours is offered in only some key categories (usually the bestselling ones). The rest of the categories are directional in offering.

While UCB is known to use many colours, classic colours dominate the product offering. Multiple colours are limited to few categories like polos, t-shirts, chinos etc. The same is true for most of such brands. Exceptions are very few and they also play out a strategy.

So, if styling tips are this clear on colour mixing and this logic is consistent across stylists, why do brands offer so many colours? Who is buying them?

But does anyone follow these 3 rules? Oh no. And why is that? Is it due to the following?

- Because we lack experience?

Most design teams are very young. While interacting with international brands, we can easily find designers in their 40's and 50's still designing. In India, is it this inexperience speaking?

- Because brands take aesthetic calls without studying and understanding colours and their impact on consumer buying?
- Because decisions about colours are left to juniors without any guidance?

How many times have we seen that after initial design approval, the additional colour-ways never come out as well?

I have spoken about 'plethora of colours' offered by brands. This brings us to an important question, one which is the premise of this article.

## How Many Colours Are Too Many?

Not sure there is an easy answer to this. It would depend on two things:

- What is your colour strategy
- How do you cluster and manage your colours by hit, flat, miss and the weightage given to those colours in similar proportion

This will automatically start rationalising the colour offering.

## A. What is your colour strategy?

The colour strategy lays the foundation of the brands' product offerings & forms the crux of its DNA. There are 2 ways to look at the strategy: **Directional & Multilateral.**

A Directional strategy is where the colour offering is limited & unified. The brand's colour story revolves around a few key colours and their tonal variations, while 1-2 experimental colours may be used as accents. This colour story is extended to all consumer touch points like advertising campaigns, VM etc. Cavin Klein & Levi's are some examples of brands built on this strategy.

A multilateral strategy is where the colours are vast with brands offering up to 25 colours in some categories. Brands in this case are identified with the colour itself and, many a times, it becomes a key story they tell. Lacoste, Desigual & UCB are some examples of brands who have adopted this strategy.

In a country like India, consumers demand variety - one that influences the businesses to shift towards the multilateral strategy.

While it may attract the consumers, it's laced with challenges. One of the biggest challenges being the rationalising of colours and creating a unified offering without making it look like a riot of colours. By '**riot of colours**', I am referring to the unplanned, unscientific use of colours.

## B. Colour clustering

As mentioned earlier, brands with a multilateral strategy should follow a category-led approach. Multi-colour offering should be limited to some key performing categories, while a directional strategy should be maintained for the other categories. For eg: Polo Ralph Lauren offers many colours in polos, but limits to fewer colours in other categories. All successful brands, with a multilateral colour offering, usually stick to this.

Another important aspect is to study the hits and misses very closely and build this strategy upwards, thus rationalising the colour range offered.

The lack of a robust colour strategy leads to an inventory pile up, making the businesses suffer.

## How Can Ignoring This Add to Financial Woes?

Let's look at a hypothetical case study.

Let's take the case of a new brand that has just launched T-Shirts in 20 fresh colours.

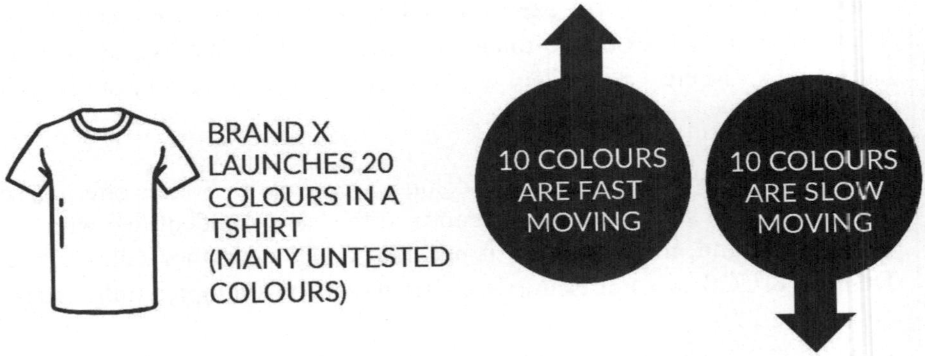


Unfortunately, the brand had to manufacture the minimum volumes basis channel and manufacturing requirements. Since, some of the colours were not well received by the consumers, the brand was saddled with inventory.

Now multiply this across categories and multiple geographical locations.

Can brand X afford to make the same mistake now?

As businesses start to scale, volumes per colour become very large making it difficult to keep introducing new untested colours as they can have huge financial implications. It can impact sell throughs, inventory, cash flows and open-to-buys - but who is listening?

I was taught early in my career to always go to the end of season sales and study the merchandise that has not sold.

And guess what! Most products were: daring colours and experimental styles in daring colours amongst the other usual suspects.

**The pertinent questions to ask would be:**

- Does anyone look at loss of sale due to incorrect colour strategy or due to the use of unrestrained colour in product lines?
- While we spend hours debating location of a store, just how much time do brand teams spend analysing colour and its impact on sales?
- Does anyone look at the cost of carrying inventory vs. the rate of sale by colour?
- Who is analysing cluster products by fast moving colours vs. fringe colour?

## Conclusion

To conclude, I would simply say:

- Learn and follow the science of colour. It can multiply sales exponentially
- Design is a marketing tool, if used properly it can do wonders for business
- Colours are simple, easier than innovation, and if managed well can have better impact on sales than any other lever. Yet companies spend endless hours focusing on getting that innovation, but how much time is spent on understanding and strategizing colour?

It's unfortunate that brands do not fully appreciate the importance of colour. Otherwise, one would see this being discussed in business meetings.

But do we? No.

Well, it's time for change, it's time to understand the true levers of the business and focus on those.

CHAPTER 2.2

# What's in a Fit?

This is another topic that's quite close to my heart. Do brands really understand the importance of fits? Can fit be a differentiator in business?

In this chapter, I will touch upon:

1. Understanding body types
2. What is a fit strategy
3. My three simple rules for fits
4. Is fit taken seriously by business
5. Benefits of having a fit strategy

## The Importance of Fits in Fashion

We all understand our own body type, and dress accordingly. Stylists from around the world urge you to dress according to your body type, yet brands do not seem to pay much heed to this.

After studying the brands in India, I realised that they think:

## India is Filled with thin People & Almost 70% of its Population is Skinny

Wondering what has led me to this conclusion?

It's the number of slim and skinny fits one sees in the market.

Usually, the brands profile the consumers to understand their requirements. They look at their income, education, age, gender etc.

But do they look at their body types?

Do we even agree that body type becomes an important aspect of consumer profiling?

It doesn't just aid in creation of the right garment and fit but also becomes a designing, marketing and positioning tool.

To understand body type, let's look at these infographics:

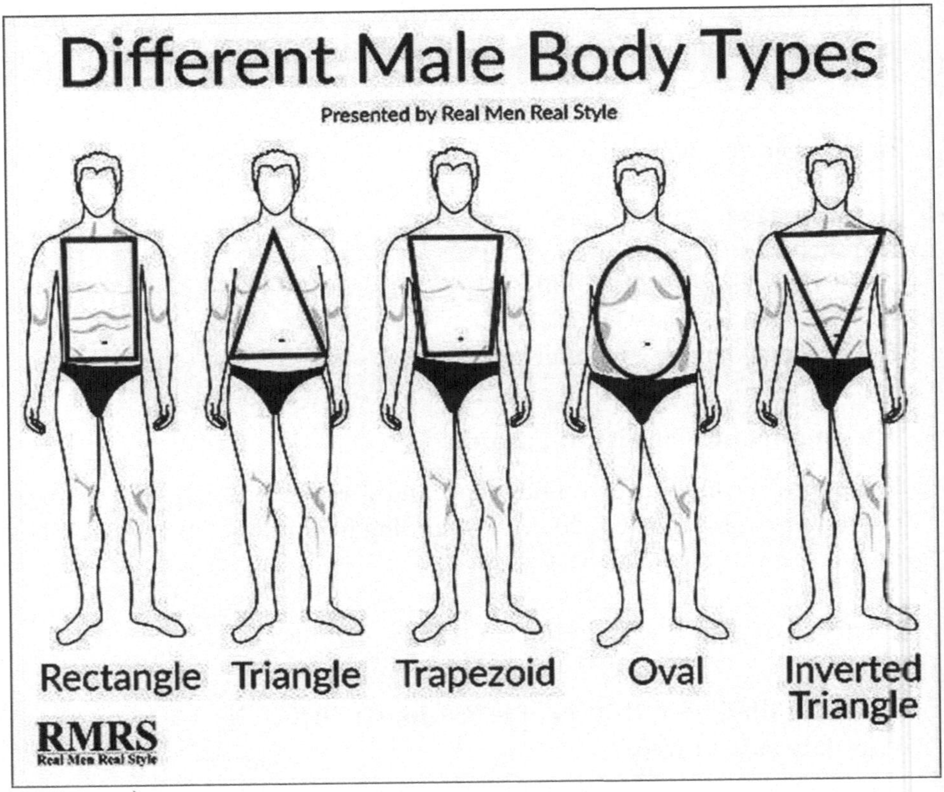


And if you thought men's body shapes are complicated, check out the women's body types -

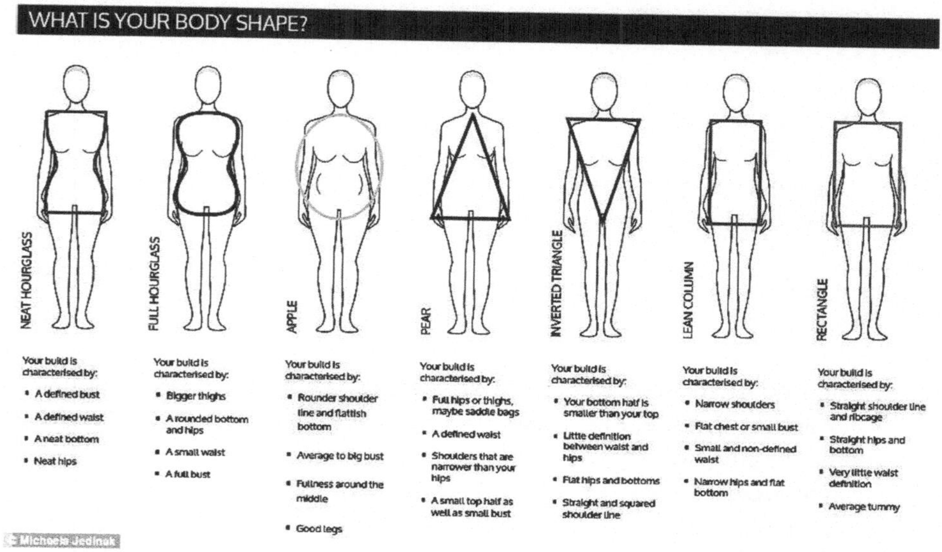


## These infographics are self-explanatory.

Have we clearly defined the body type for those buying our clothes? The first rule of marketing is - know your customer. Well, do we?

And that is the question I am asking?

Having understood the above body type segmentation, I would like to ask the reader if they can tell which brands are catering to which of the body types? Is it clear in their communication? Are their charts mapping fits to body types in the store for ease of buying or have you, after many mistrials, started to make a beeline for the few brands that actually fit your body type well?

Many international brands build their fits around a specific target audience based on their body types.

And this leads me to the next segment.

## What is a Fit Strategy?

It's surprising that 'Fit' is often ignored by fashion and retail businesses in India.

The pertinent questions brands need to ask themselves are:

- Who is buying from me?
- Age, Gender, **Body type**?
- Size analysis?
- Sales loss due to fit/size issue?
- How is this data captured?

Once this is clear, brands need to clearly establish a fit strategy. These can be of 3 types:

1. **Focused fit strategy** where a brand targets a single body type and makes clothes for them. For eg: if one goes to Zara, it's clearly targeted towards a slim & petite body type.
2. **Segmented fit strategy** where a brand targets multiple body types for key categories and those are available in multiple fits and sizes. All other categories are managed through generic fits where, with fewer fits and sizes, brands accommodate more body types.
3. **Generic fit strategy** where brand tries to accommodate as many body types as possible by offering fits and sizes that are more generic. This allows them to address a larger segment of consumers while having fewer fits and sizes. Typically, family stores follow this strategy.

Having discussed possible fit strategies, let's now talk about: **My 3 Simple Rules for Fits**, which have evolved over time. I am sharing it with the hope that our readers will benefit from these.

### Fit rule number 1: In a brand, the same size should fit the consumer across all products & fits.

Make life simple for the consumer. In most brands, if a 'M' size, in regular fit, works for the consumer, he has to force himself to wear a 'L' size in slim fit. Why? For the consumer, if she/he wears a 'M' in a brand, she/he should be able to wear 'M' across all their products. It saves time on mistrial and retrial making it easy for the consumer to pick clothes without really trying them on as she/he is confident of the fit.

### Fit rule number 2: Use standardised body forms and models for fit trials.

Standardise the base body measurements for the brand, develop body forms and use those for fit trials. Even if we keep a panel of live models, please ensure they are the right body types and measurements.

There is a tendency for the designers, buyers, and business heads to try the garments on themselves and personalise it to their own bodies. The brand must ensure it fits their consumer profile and should discourage teams from these 'personalised' fit approvals. If they binged at a party the night before trying a fitted garment, without a doubt the fit will go for a retrial.

Standardisation of these processes is of the utmost importance.

### Fit rule number 3: Clearly define where to go for fitted garments and where to go with generic fits.

Fitted garments require more sizes, more variants. This increases inventory holding as number of sizes and fits that need to be managed goes up. Generic fits can easily be designed which are roomier and allow a higher number of body types to fit into, with lesser number of sizes, hence, reducing inventory risk.

Now, every brand needs to look at this clearly in terms of which categories they want to invest into more sizes and where they want to offer width.

But this is all common knowledge. So, why don't we find brands focusing on clearly defined fit strategy? What ails us?

### Is Fit taken seriously by businesses?

Every fit decision is an investment decision, yet what is the infrastructure we have built in our companies to get good quality fits? Do we benchmark, analyse, study consumer reaction to fits, invest in quality technicians, fit testing softwares, body forms, pattern making and sampling infrastructure to ensure that no stone is left unturned to ensure consumer delight?

Fits are clearly investment calls. The money invested in a fit is much more than the money spent on acquiring stores - but store acquisition may take up a lot more top management time than deciding on a fit strategy or finalising a fit into which crores would be invested in the form of inventory.

Most brands do not have a well-articulated fit strategy and leave it to designers and product teams, at mid to junior levels, to do that. And this leads to 'fit personalisation'.

I remember being in a panel discussion where a department store chain MD was lamenting about the fact that in his own store, he could not buy most of the products as they were in slim fits, and it did not fit him.

He made a very interesting point that India has a large population and is capable of discretionary spend in the mid to older ages, but no one designs for them. The point is that brands need to move to a clearly defined or differentiated fit strategy. This will lead to some major benefits as I have enumerated below.

## Benefits Of Having a Well-Articulated Fit Strategy

### Consumer Loyalty

I have been in many discussions and meetings on consumer loyalty. But the unfortunate truth is that in fashion, most companies seem to overlook the obvious. The biggest hook for consumer loyalty, in clothing, is fit.

Once consumers like a fit, they just keep going back for it. Look at how Levi's has created their consumer loyalty on fits, some of them going back decades. They may play within the fits, but fundamentally give the consumers jeans that fit well.

In fact, in stores, you can see consumers asking, 'can you show me some new options in this fit?' They are so sure of the fit that they buy it even without trying. That's the power of loyalty.

It's amazing how fits can define the fortunes of a fashion brand.

## Lower Returns in E-commerce

With e-commerce increasing in scale and size, brands need to take fit-standardisation and strategy very seriously. How they communicate, the consistency of sizing across brand products, all will have a huge impact on returns, trials and consumer time. The brands need to decide how important their consumer experience is for them.

Once consumers start trusting the sizing and fits of a brand, they will start ordering with more faith which can have an exponential impact on sales. But this requires, well defined fit strategy, consistency and clear communication.

## Differentiation

Fit can be a major differentiator in business. Particularly category-focused brands could have a field day with it. It is something which is a clear differentiator. A brand that makes great looking clothes may attract the consumers, but a brand that makes good looking and great fitting clothes will convert the consumer to a brand loyalist. Isn't that what we all want?

## Conclusion

To conclude, I would only say that fashion brands, including retailers, need to clearly understand who their consumers are and make a fit strategy to suit them.

In Europe and the US, there are a host of new brands catering to fashion for heavier women. This is because they felt embarrassed to try on clothes in stores and not fit into them. These brands understood their customers' body types & started catering to them.

Sometimes, we are looking at so many reasons for why sales are declining and walk-ins, reducing. But very few realise that selling ill-fitted clothes is a silent killer. The consumer just walks away, and we don't even realise why.

I am amazed at the kind of trivia that passes for reportage in the industry, but no one understands or discusses real issues the industry is facing.

CHAPTER 2.3

# Is Fashion Design Commercial Art or Fine Art?

This is the third article in the '**Myths in Fashion Design**' series. We have already covered colours and fits in my previous chapters. In this final edition, I will talk about a much-misunderstood issue in fashion - Is Fashion Design a commercial or fine art?

In this chapter, I will talk about:

- Why the ambiguity
- How to align commerce with aesthetics
- My three simple rules for design
- Benefits of driving a commercial design team

For this article, we will be discussing **'designing'** in the context of mass brands and not couture. So, let's move to our first topic.

## Why is there ambiguity?

I always felt that it comes from the lack of understanding of which business function entails the design aspect. But it really hit home, one day, when I realised that business teams are mostly ignorant of the fact that their indecisiveness and last-minute changes on the production lines, lead to delays and cost escalations.

Their point is: Design is an art form, and they are producing works of art and, hence, indecision and changes even on the factory floor is okay because at the end of the day, it must come out 'perfect'.

Well, how does one define '**perfection**' in the commercial context?

So, this brings me to the '***mera wala* pink**' syndrome.

Everyone who has submitted multiple lab dips will understand what I am talking about. Invariably, we come across designers who reject multiple submissions based on what's in their minds, or because it does not match the said Pantone perfectly. But does the consumer know this?

All he/she sees is what's on the shop floor and decides if he/she likes it or not. Unfortunately, I have witnessed endless arguments on this aspect from both sides of the table.

I remember a case where the designer rejected 5 submissions and I happened to be in on the 6th approval discussion. She was at pains to describe the 'pink' in a baby's palm for which she could not find a perfect Pantone reference. Unfortunately, no one around could also get the right pink, and so was coined the '*mera wala* pink' syndrome.

In my understanding, the problem lies in the misalignment of a designer's expectation vs a consumer's expectation. A consumer doesn't know what Pantone the designer wanted; they only know if they like the product. Hence, I say commercial designers need to take commercial calls. Ensure that the end product is aesthetic and saleable, even if it's not '*mera wala* pink'.

## So, then what is the designer supposed to bring to the table?

- Ability to visualise
- Ability to translate that vision and articulate it with tangible tools like Pantones, tech packs, fabrics, and patterns to enable other stakeholders to clearly understand what is required
- Ability to look at products from a consumers' lens
- Ability to be consistent with brand's visual and creative direction
- Quick decision-making and closure and not get carried away with the myriad possibilities that exist

## This job is made harder because,

- A designer's work is always judged by others, and this heightens the fear of failure in them
- Everybody has a point of view on design

There is always an aura around designers that makes them look like they are from another planet. While I will not comment on why that happens, the reality is that it does. Many a times, this leads to designers not interacting with the rest of the stakeholders the way they should. The different functions also create an enigma around them, resulting in business teams finding it hard to relate to design teams.

How then should they objectively set expectations?

Here are my **3 simple rules for Commercialising Design Teams**.

**Rule No. 1**

Being on time and good is better than being late but perfect.

'*It's better to be roughly right than perfectly wrong*', quoting Keynes in a design chapter. Ah! The cost of perfection. Michelangelo took 12 years to create the *Sistine Chapel* but are we creating that one perfect piece or ensuring that the right merchandise reaches the consumer at the right time. 'The cost of being late versus the pleasure of being perfect', is the eternal ambiguity.

**Rule No. 2**

Design to cost, keeping the commerce in commercial art.

A huge amount of time is wasted by businesses in getting this right. So, working out the basic raw material components and their costs, and aligning it to business requirement before designing with those, is the key to successful commercial design.

**Rule No. 3**

Create marketing stories around product lines.

Most consumers buy products, not ensembles and looks. A lot of time and effort goes into creating differentiated design and products, but are these marketing ideas? Brands and their products need to tell a story, give a reason to the consumer to buy them. Everyone makes great products these days, have good aesthetics as well, but it's the brands that successfully tell their stories that win in the end.

So, to answer the question on how to align is simple:

- Develop a clear understanding of what the design function is supposed to bring to the table
- Set clear expectations based on the above 3 rules
- Allow a set percentage of the business to be steered through experimentation by the creative design teams; this should be their window of creativity beyond the defined set

## And finally, what's the benefit of driving design in the above fashion

This is the simplest one to answer, really.

- **Speed to Market** dramatically goes up if design teams are aligned. It is this tug of war between designers' ask and commercial viability that takes up to 6 weeks in the development process
- **Profitability Soars** when commercials are aligned from concept to wardrobe
- **Sell-throughs increase and the brand scores** when designers think marketing stories rather than purely aesthetic concepts

## Conclusion

Design forms the foundation of any business, and an empowered design team becomes a big asset to the company as is evident from the benefits mentioned earlier.

Commercial design and designers have to re-look at the conventional ways in which they function and evolve into a business specific role. While creativity is the central premise of a design team and its objectives, it's also important to align with the business outputs. After all, the success of a commercial designer lies in the success of the business at large.

**Let's look at some key points I would like to leave the readers with:**

- Designers should continue to pursue their creative endeavours but with a purpose in mind. If a designer is working for a brand, it's important for him/her to work differently and add these skills to his/her repertoire.
- Designers need to go beyond what they are doing and evolve into successful designers by understanding the business models, along with tweaking their output to better suit them.
- Commercial design comes with many constraints. A smart designer will be able to understand these and work around them in creative ways. Designers in couture labels are very different in this respect. They are creating art and selling one piece of each, while commercial designers are making mass produced garments which must be liked by many, one that needs to fit into competitive costing models and be feasible for mass manufacture. Brands need them to work differently and need practical minds to lead the aesthetic and technical aspects of the products & design based on that.

Designers are the foundation of a business, and if the foundation is strong, businesses flourish.

CHAPTER 2.4

# Are Seasons Relevant in Fashion Anymore?

This is a very controversial topic and not one that's easy to write about. So, when I volunteered to write on this, I had no idea of what I was getting into. I don't even think anyone believes there is an issue here. Then why was this troubling me? Well, let's see if I can influence you on this.

In this feature, I will talk about whether '**Seasons**' as a concept is relevant anymore in the fashion retail industry by understanding:

- The genesis and evolution of seasons as a concept in fashion
- Is this one of the reasons for the retail apocalypse?
- Have seasons become a noose around our neck?
- How should we look at the business going forward?

Let's look at the seasons as we understand them.

To the world, these words denote weather patterns, but to everyone in the fashion industry, it's a way of life. Seasons are ingrained into every process in our supply chain. A designer designs as per seasons, buyer's OTB is seasonal, sales plans are seasonal, so on and so forth.

## But are they relevant anymore?

To answer this question, we need to first understand the genesis and evolution of seasons.

## The Genesis And Evolution of 'Seasons'

In the fashion industry, the concept of seasons started because people needed season-relevant clothing due to the extremities in weather conditions. Warm clothing was a winter necessity and soft breathable fabrics, a summer.

Back then, clothes were considered essentials or a necessity. But all that changed when the world saw economic development. As more and more people became economically empowered and affluent, clothing moved from necessity to fashion.

The industrial revolution created large factories to mass-produce clothing and then came brands that wanted to increase per capita consumption. To that end, they started promoting fashion as clothes that needed to change every season. From the silhouettes to colours, something new was offered every season. What the consumers wore the previous season was denounced as redundant a few months later. Brands primarily dictated what was in trend and told the consumers what to wear and what to discard.

The whole idea was to promote more and more buying. And boy, did we succeed! Between 2000 and 2014, clothing production doubled **with the average consumer buying 60 per cent more pieces of garment compared to 15 years ago**. Consumers in the United Kingdom have an estimated **US $ 46.7 billion worth of unworn clothes in their closets.**

Over some time, this got adopted into the DNA of the fashion industry. Research developed on how to make seasons work for fashion. The whole supply chain from 'yarn to brands' calendarised this. Retailers started buying as per this - trade shows followed, marketing calendars, design, innovation and even ERP systems hardcoded this.

In the meantime, a curious thing was happening in the industry...

Is this one of the reasons for the retail apocalypse in the last decade?

The last decade has been devastating to the American retail industry as traditional malls and countless brands continued to shutter at record highs, some of them being iconic and heritage brands. **As many as 9,300 stores closed in 2019, while 1.3 million jobs have disappeared during the last 10 years in the US alone**.

There are many reasons attributed to this – most important being the 'onset of online platforms' amongst others. But can we just pause to consider these few other points like, inefficient inventory, built by incorrect sales forecasting, necessitated by long product lead times, led by a seasonal calendar, followed across the industry?

But this brings us to where we started.

Have seasons become a noose around our neck?

Seasons were simply supposed to be 'go-to-market' periods, with new products to compel consumers to buy more. But they have taken a life of their own and become an immortal edifice to the art of storytelling.

Unfortunately, trade shows, retail buying, design cycles, marketing and innovation calendars are all bound to this seasonal logic and do not consider, category nuances and supply chain logic. Instead, they apply seasonality to everything. Lack of transparency in supply chains has led to retailers using similar inventory norms for core, bestsellers, and fashion. For example, even if core could be replenished every week, retailers keep 8-12 weeks of inventory, just to be sure that they don't run dry. This seasonal approach pushes the store to refresh 70 per cent+ of their merchandise every season. This forecast and push-based supply chain led to designing and planning 6-12 months in advance. Production commitments were made months before the consumer even saw the product.

This has led to **over forecasting and inefficient inventory planning. Discounting & Liquidation** became another menace the industry had to deal with, sometimes having to even burn the unsold inventory. These became large looming problems for the industry, which led to the unravelling of these fashion bigwigs.

Has the seasonal DNA of the industry become obsolete?

To answer that we need to figure out what happened to sales? If traditional brands and retailers were collapsing, did this mean that people were buying fewer clothes this decade?

Well, people are still buying the same amount of clothes, if not more. This only meant that there was a shift in 'where' the consumers were buying from.

Then the next logical question would be:

How should we look at the business going forward?

To understand this, we need to study the new kids on the block.

Let's look at some of the new businesses that have come up like ASOS, Boohoo, Myntra and many such online platforms. These were primarily tech-companies, which disregarded the seasonal approach. They focused on understanding consumer behaviour on the tech platforms, buying patterns, data mining and last-mile connectivity. Their focus was on developing products that sold, challenging the status quo. They would introduce a product, monitor its rate of sale, and then decide how much more to make. Even the frequency of product introduction was different. The consumer bought when he wanted, not waiting for seasons and brand directions on trends.

Social media had changed the consumer forever. Brands needed to reimagine their relevance to consumers, who started looking at a multitude of influences beyond trend forecasts by fashion brands. Having lost the ability to influence trends like in the old days, brands that were following this seasonal go-to-market with forecast and push-based sales, started collapsing.

And brands that did not follow seasons and just tapped into consumer demands started flourishing. If you don't believe me, just Google the list of brands that filed for insolvency in the States during the last decade!

The question that we therefore need to ask is – should we not look at different businesses, channels and events and work on go-to-market cycles independent of seasons? This would then mean:

- Building 'go-to-market' calendars differently for different categories, keeping in mind supply chain nuances, lead times and planning inventory basis that.
- Building the business calendar around events, festivals, seasons with equal fervour. Design and plan around these events. Many brands look at these as flash buys that are not part of the mainstream buys.
- De-risk inventory by reducing season refresh percentages and moving to a clear try and repeat strategy.
- Bring focus to replenishment business.

If we look around, we will see a lot of category-based brands and manufacturer brands who have started to play this game, and quite successfully so.

I leave you with the premise that 'seasons' as the industry DNA is obsolete. The consumer has moved on. Should we also not do the same?

Do share your thoughts with me and our readers, as this is a topic that requires more exhaustive debate.

CHAPTER 2.5

# Do We Really Understand Innovation?

The word '**Innovation**' has become a mainstay in our lives. Many industries have seen a drastic change in the past few years owing to this and the fashion industry has felt this change too.

Lycra by DuPont, AIRism by Uniqlo, Levi's Commuter series, Boost by Adidas are a few examples of brands defining innovations. Consumers instantly associate these products with their respective brands. And that's the 'Power of Innovation'.

With so many new innovations being tried out each season, fashion is one of the most innovative industries, yet only a few innovations come to mind when we think hard – like something big that became a trend or changed the industry.

In this feature, I will discuss what innovation really means to consumers through the below sections:

- Innovation and its definition
- Innovation in the fashion industry
- Innovation from the consumers' lens
- Innovation and where it gets lost between all the stakeholders

**But what does innovation mean?**

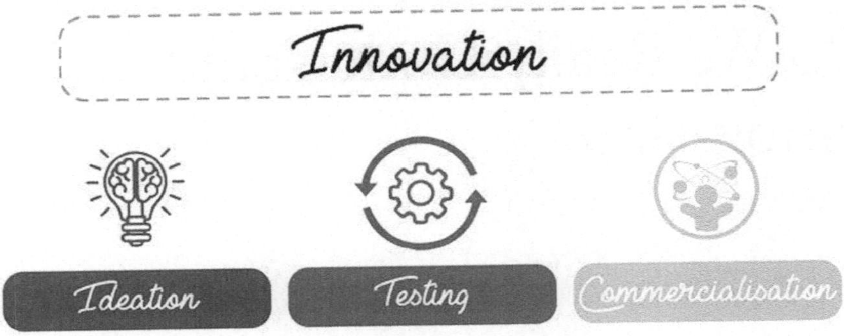


*original infographic created by Aninyda Ray

While this definition stays true to the fashion industry too, we need to look at innovation with a more specialised industry lens. It can be defined as a multi-stage process whereby organisations transform ideas into new/improved products, service, or processes, to advance, compete and differentiate themselves successfully in their marketplace.

The fashion industry is a fragmented one. There are many stakeholders in the supply chain – farmers growing cotton, the spinning units making yarn, weavers converting yarn to fabrics, processing units and mills making this fabric wearable, the garmenting units creating the final piece of clothing, and finally the brands and retailers who brand and sell the same to us, the consumers.

In this landscape, consisting of so many stakeholders and each trying to innovate and do something different, it is very important to understand what is relevant for the final consumer. **Do we really understand innovation** or are we simply innovating for the sake of innovating to convince the stakeholder next in the pipeline to select our product over the competition, since we promise either better performance with incremental improvement in parameters or better cost for the same consumer's benefit?

We have seen many innovations in the recent past. From fabrics with inherent antimicrobial properties to speciality yarns that save water, fabrics that regulate body temperature, colours that never fade, washes which use zero water and so on…

But the fundamental question I ask here is:

Does the consumer understand these innovations? What do these innovations mean to the consumer? When he/she walks into the store, or logs onto a website, what are they looking for?

**<u>The answer to this question is:</u>**

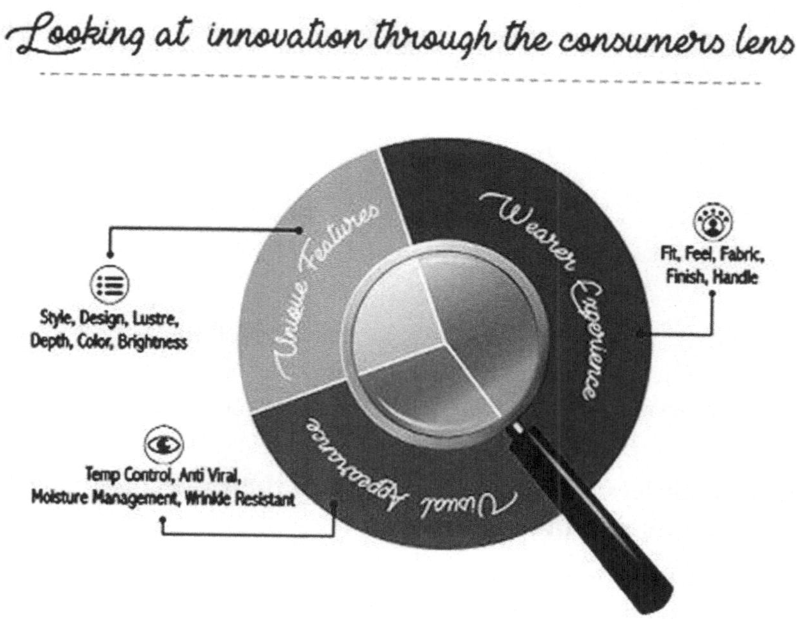


*original infographic created by Aninyda Ray

Consumers look at garments very differently from the technocrats in the industry. From wearer experience to visual appearance and finally unique features, each matter, but in different measures as is evident from the graphic below.

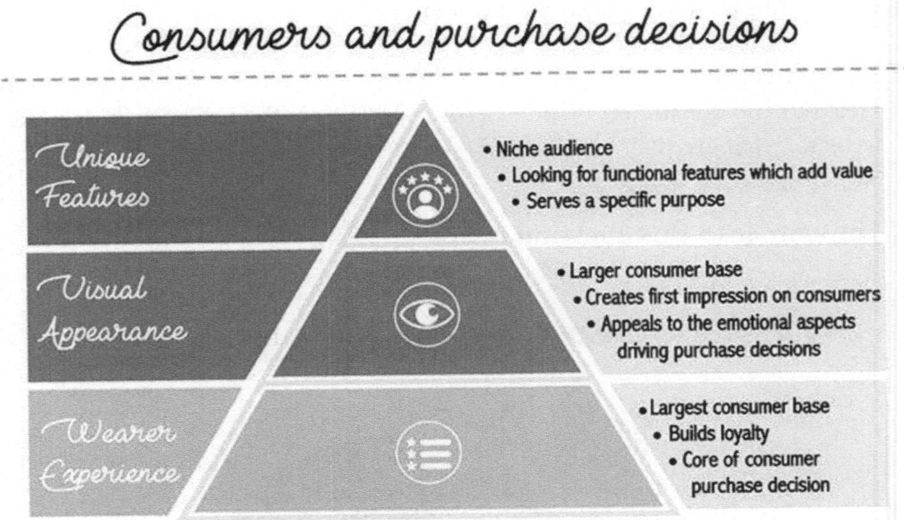


*original infographic created by Aninyda Ray

Unfortunately, aspects of the business that impact the largest consumer segments are usually the ones which get the least focus from the businesses. People seem to focus on aspects which drive niche audience.

## How does understanding consumers and their purchase decisions help us understand innovations?

It is simple. Look at innovation from the consumers' lens. If it makes sense to the consumer and drives them to buy the product, then the innovation and the effort behind it is worthwhile.

It is very easy to get swayed by the sheer number of innovations taking place on a daily basis. Everyone around us is innovating, yarns to fabrics to trims to finishes… fibre with a hollow core, foam dyes, silicon washing chemicals, so on and so forth.

We get so lost in the business-to-business branding and in incremental numbers that we forget the most important person – the consumer. How is he/she looking at this innovation?

Are the consumers understanding the benefits of these innovations? What does it mean to them?

A lot of effort goes into innovation, but unfortunately most of it goes waste because businesses are not focusing on the final consumer benefit. They are happy chasing incremental increase in parameters and their supply chain customers, hardly focusing on the final consumer.

And this is the fundamental problem we need to understand.

## How should the various stakeholders look at innovation?

Here is a simplified example of what innovation can mean for the **3 most important components** in our industry namely yarn, fabric and garmenting. The important thing being, how is every stakeholder understanding final consumer benefit.

Stakeholders and Innovations

| | Yarn | Fabric | Garmenting |
|---|---|---|---|
| Wearer Experience | - Soft and pliable<br>- Unique Blends | - Handfeel<br>- Shape Retention | - Good fits<br>- Drape and fall |
| Visual Appearance | - Clean Surface Appearance<br>- No pilling | - Brightness & Lustre<br>- Sharp Optics | - Styling<br>- Surface Embellishments<br>- Washes & Finishes |
| Unique Features | - Sustainable Sources<br>- Hollow Core Yarn<br>- High Stretch | - Medicinal Finishes<br>- Moisture Management<br>- Performance Finishes | - Built-in Ear Phones<br>- Biometric Sensing |

*original infographic created by Aninyda Ray

Brands and retailers are closest to the consumers. It is they who market the end product.

When Adidas launched Boost, it changed the company's fortune. People knew the brand, but Boost gave them a reason to choose Adidas over its competitors. Similarly, look at Levi's commuter series, an innovation that combined many innovative components into a product beneficial to the consumers.

That is why there are a few examples of successful innovations, though the industry comes up with new ones almost every day. This is also because innovations have been turned into fashion. The market is flooded with minor innovations promising incremental benefit or a certain niche.

Unfortunately, these are not marketed strongly either. Hence the pressure to keep innovating leads to a number game that keeps businesses turning out innovation after innovation without looking through the consumers' lens.

To conclude, I will reiterate that each stakeholder needs to look at innovation from a consumers' point of view.

- It is imperative that the whole supply chain is involved in understanding innovation as it should be from the consumers' lens. The yarn manufacturer, the fabric manufacturers and all other stakeholders should understand innovation and consumer benefit.
- Rather than too many innovations, one should focus on few but clearly differentiated ones which are easily understood by the consumers.
- Market them properly and be consistent in driving that innovation year-on-year. Simply put, if the brand doesn't believe in it beyond a season, why should the consumer?

Having written about different aspects of innovation, I urge everyone to think about innovations in this new light and then decide whether it should be innovation for the sake of innovation or innovation that has relevant consumer benefits.

CHAPTER 2.6

# From The Readers' Mind!

We, at **Inside Apparel**, take pride in being a platform where you, the readers, can express, discuss, opine & share your points of views.

Each article on this site has garnered multi-faceted comments, many of which are thought provoking & intriguing. With each opinion expressed, we all learn something new & insightful.

We are sharing some of these opinions & comments from **The Myths In Fashion Design Series.** We are unable to represent every comment here but would urge you to read through them at leisure.

**The Myths In Fashion Design** series consists of 3 articles:

1. How many colours are too many colours?
2. What is in a fit?
3. Is Fashion Design Commercial or Fine art?

Now let's look at the varied comments posted by our readers! Enjoy the insights...

## BUILDING BLOCKS OF A BRAND

*"An architecture of buying - selecting the blocks to make a brand, to give it a personality, be it Directional or Multilateral, is the primary step in the visualisation of a brand.* ***There is a science behind colours and selling pattern*** *- to study that is important and give us insights like blue is the new black or green sells!!!"*

- Sarika Arora, Corporate sales head, Royal Data Matics Pvt. Ltd.

## COLOURS & SELL THROUGH'S - A UNIQUE CORRELATION

*"Colours --the perpetual discussion. The reality is that it be menswear or womenswear ---there is core colour palette. It can change region to region with an accent but there definitely is a core colour range which sells. In a fashion brand, there has to be a core and some accent colours, based on the season's forecasts. These are only fillers or for the look---this will never be the major sale. There was one brand which used to put black in every style and allow the designer to choose the other colour from the colour palette. This simple ploy used to drive up their sell-through per style. There are others who advise that core colours must have larger quantities and accent colours must have smaller buys. It's the ones who allow equal buys in all colours of the colour palette who end up with the stocks.* ***I've worked with the 7 top known brands of the world and found that their understanding of colour is what made half the sell through****. This is indeed an interesting discussion".*

- Poonam Sood Lal, Consultant, Co-Founder Sash Exports (Buying House)

## EXPERIENCE SAYS IT ALL

*"And this point is very true, that why we don't follow these rules --- because we lack experience?* ***Most design teams are very young. Interacting with international brands, you can easily find designers in their 40's and 50's still designing****. In India, is it this inexperience speaking?"*

- Swati Sriram, Design Consultant (Apparel and Home furnishing)

## COLORS BEYOND DESIGNERS

*"Very important topic and very well explained.* ***I agree with you completely as these are the very basic principles of color play. I believe, most of the experienced designers do understand this and this should be a quintessential subject for Product Merchandisers and Sales managers also to study****. I completely agree that a successful brand is successful because of the strategy it plans & follows. I hope this article is read by all in the retail industry, understood and well implemented too".*

- Prasenjit Adhikari, Creative Director Arrow @ Arvind brands

## ROOT CAUSE ANALYSIS

*"The conclusion on* ***sales loss would definitely require a root cause analysis****. Every EOSS has numerous reasons and I find one to be the choice of colors. We*

*might think those as the best sellers and aren't. This will improve the designers' capabilities and correlate to customers' choice".*

- Shankar

## STANDARDISE FITS & HOW

*"In the domestic business I've seen designers trying styles on themselves and commenting. This is absolutely unacceptable. In international business, the dummy and fit model are standardised and no one can tamper with it.*

*The question then comes –* ***how to standardise a fit in India? Take your top 3 selling brands – study their fits and take the top 3 street side brands (critical to do this) and study their fit.*** *The street side brands would actually know the customer better, otherwise they will simply lose the customer as most do not have fitting rooms.* ***Do NOT try to invent the wheel by introducing new fits.***

*The fit is the most critical part of the garment. We allow designers to tamper with it. It must stop. With standardised fits, everyone can concentrate on the design element from the factory to the ultimate customer".*

- Poonam Sood Lal, Consultant, Co-Founder Sash Exports (Buying House)

## FIT COMES FIRST

*"Thank you for enumerating most important part of a garment which is fit.* ***The process of fit development is extremely important and difficult part of a brand.*** *But once it is cracked one should also maintain and update according to changing customer preference. Any fit the customer should feel comfortable, then the look and style".*

- Prashanth HV, Product Strategy, Royal Enfield Apparel

## GOOD FIT EQUALS LOYALTY

*"The biggest hook for consumer loyalty in clothing is FIT of the garment.* ***I agree that sales will multiply exponentially once customers start trusting the size and fit of a brand.*** *Customers getting discouraged when their actual size do not fit for other brands. Nowadays, customers are using various online platforms to buy their merchandise where they can't do any wear-trial, in that case fit standardisation and fit strategy play a vital role. And you very well explained that whether online or offline purchase, great fitting clothes will convert the consumers to a brand loyalist.* ***By understanding their consumer's body types,***

***study consumer reactions to fit, brands can ensure their consumer delight, otherwise the investment will end up into inventory only".***

- Ravindra Chawla, Operations Head - Quality at Arvind Lifestyle Brands Ltd

## FIT IS TECHNICAL

*"I agree with you on the approach towards handling fits by most of the brands and retailers in India. Many brands don't really go through the process and the time taken for a fit creation. Either it is copied or tweaked from popular fits in trend. Like colours, fabrics, cost and brands, fit is very personalised experience of a consumer. Having standardised 'M' or 'L' across the fits might be challenging especially when the target customers' age group is wider.* ***Developing a fit without compromising wearer's comfort defines the success of it. While developing the fit, we should know the purpose, target group, body anatomy and contours of gender and age groups of the specific geographical region.*** *Creating a good fit begins here without having answers for these questions may not yield the desirable results. And developing a good fit is science - having said that, right technical skill set, and resources are important. This is really understood and implemented well in the fashion industry in western hemisphere. Here, we still contemplate with it and considered to manage on the go. Imparting the basic knowledge of fits and development process is essential to the PD, product, sourcing, and buyers".*

- Ramesh Ramalingam, VP Sourcing Operations, Arvind Fashions

## FIT IS A PART OF RANGE CONSTRUCT

*"I read the article couple of times to understand the 'need for a FIT STRATEGY for a brand or retailer separated from the product strategy. I completely agree that FIT is one of the most important criterias for a product purchase. Having said that I believe,* ***a good product/ Buying manager must embed Fit as part of the range construct. The basic premises of understanding the customer and the brand proposition, range construct would take care of category offering, fabric & colour selection, fit offering, and pricing****. Depending upon the consumer buying behaviour, each category has its selection criteria - how well the buyer is able to map and align the offering to this, makes him/ her good or bad.*

*Alienating Slim/Skinny fit in favour of Comfort fit may not be the answer. With the whole fitness movement from gyms & fitness centres, healthy eating options, mind and body wellness programs, that have fuelled the Fitness & Sports industry, workout is becoming a part of average Indian.*

*Investing in studies and Fit researches, consumer fit testing is a better approach. Quality of fit technicians, investing in training a buyer & designer to understand how basic measurement, cuts and shaping could evolve into a desirable and well-accepted fit.*

**At Meraki, we understood Fit to be our most important component, we have ergonomically designed our silhouettes and fits to ensure they drape and fit well on various body shapes. Our floating size concept takes care of the 'in betweens' and caters to a huge 'not-so-perfect' body types.** *Being an e-commerce womenswear brand, by investing in identifying the right fit for our customer has kept our returns to a bare 6% as against 30% industry norm and our customer repeat purchase is 45%. It's a different but complimenting perspective on the article, the teams to work their skills on bettering the RANGE CONSTRUCT. Thank you Anindya for bringing these insights and initiating the dialogues with readers for all rounded views".*

- Himanshu Singh, Co-founder, Meraki

## LACK OF STANDARD MEASUREMENTS

*"Unlike Europe, Australia, Japan, USA –* ***India still has not derived a standard measurement chart****. With our diversified cultures and regions, the scope of FIT or measurements becomes very critical for any launch. Thus, we majorly attribute the fits based on running trends. If we look at the return stocks, we can easily analyze the sale trend. The question is are we doing this?"*

- Ajay Ravuri, General Manager, Quality @ Arvind Fashions Limited

## SUBJECT MATTER EXPERT NEEDED

*"There is enough data to retrieve the standard sizes from sale's history.* ***However, I'd like to stress that this area requires a 'Subject Matter Expert' and strong technical know-how & intervention.***

*I spent my initial years in M&S, working as a technician, and learnt that fit is not just an outcome of a correct size chart, it requires technical skill and mastery. An almost perfect fit requires:*

- *Basic construction guidelines*
- *Deep understanding of fabric behavior*
- *Standard size mannequins*
- *Understanding in pattern making*
- *Draping skills*
- *Understanding in sewing, ease, allowance etc.*

*There's plenty that goes into getting a fit right.*

*Designers & Brands must not take decisions on fits on their own, as it's not their area of expertise, they must, at all times, seek informed decisions from technical experts".*

- Neeraj Katoch, Sr. Mgr B&M, Arvind Fashions

## LEAP TOWARDS TECHNOLOGY

*"Fit is paramount in decision-making but also in customer loyalty, as you rightly said. Hopefully we are going to take a* ***leap towards technology as an industry and will be able to answer the question 'what's in a fit?'*** *with 'Everything' soon".*

- Nitin Gupta, Design, Innovation & BD at Arvind Ltd.

## DATA & FACTS - PARAMOUNT IMPORTANCE

***"Diligent data mining and fact finding on consumers across physical parameters.*** *Consumer insighting across emotional parameters have a huge impact on off take. Should be taken very seriously".*

- Karunesh Vir Vohra, Catalyst @ Business of Design at BO

## MERA WALA PINK SYNDROME

*"I can't agree more than this with you. It's an amazing series with 360 degree insights of all the fundamental aspects of our trade. As I was part of many such conversations with design team, I exactly know what is 'Mera wala pink syndrome'.* ***Imparting the knowledge of apparel manufacturing processes and most importantly the timelines with design team are imperative.*** *There should always be a balance between creativity and commerciality. I had seen designers who are very decisive, having strong commercial sense and upholding the brand DNA all the time".*

- Ramesh Ramalingam, VP Sourcing Operations, Arvind Fashions

*"Your observation on The Mera Wala Pink syndrome is hilarious and so true. I admit, I have done this too but later, better sense prevailed, and I learnt that it's important to have a bird's eye view and a wider understanding of the brands or business requirement.*

***I have also noticed that a lot of apparel designers bring in their personal tastes and preferences, losing sight of brand handwriting, positioning, and pricing".***

- Moutushi Dey, Design Consultant

## A FASHION DESIGNER OR AN APPAREL DESIGNER?

*"I see these as two separate things.*

*Fashion designing is the art of designing clothing, fashion, accessories, etc.*

***Apparel designing is a more technical term–pertaining to the specific act of creating clothing from nuts to bolts. If someone is apparel designing, I see them more as a technician.*** *For example, when a big house hires a team of designers to create a line under that house's label such as Puma or Nike or Gap, those designers, who work for that house, would be referred to as apparel designers.*

*In order to bring speed to market, a brand, while hiring, should be clear on their requirements.*

*Does their business permit to hire Fashion Designer or Apparel Designer?"*

- Sanjay Lal, Co-founder, Sash Exports (Buying House)

## A COMMERCIAL DESIGNER

*"The transition from an artist to a designer starts with fashion education. The growth from a designer to a commercial designer is helped by acquiring technical, functional and production knowledge of product one works with. But to top it off and be really successful as a commercial designer, one needs to layer all the technical and production knowledge over a culture of imbibing the brand DNA (also called the brand signature/ design language etc).* ***When one can seamlessly transition from concept to sample to production feasibility, incorporate top quality parameters into the final product, work with the production planning team to ensure best bulk output and finally also articulate how would it be displayed/catalogued, communicated/described and price it most effectively for a high sales velocity (effectively is not about being the lowest MRP achievable at a certain multiple but about fitting in with customer and pricing trends for similar brands).*** *A designer's mind needs to move from concept to revenue per option through the stages of shortlisting and finalizing, ruthlessly. Emotions have a role to play for most designers, right brained as they are. It's a fine balance most designers will need to strike, and once they're able to balance their emotions and commercial pragmatism, a designer is probably the biggest asset an organisation has, and the glue that keeps buying, merchandising, sourcing and retail planning stuck together on a journey to greatness".*

- Gautam Kotmraju, former Co-founder at CultSport, CultGear

## CONCLUSION

Design lays the foundation of any apparel business. They are entrusted with bringing the brand alive and design clothes which don't just look good, but also make the customers come back again and again.

With a systematic thought-through approach, as suggested in these articles, the design team will deliver business results and keep the customers coming back for more.

While there are a few notions which suggest otherwise, it's important that the designers prioritise and look at the bigger picture.

I hope you enjoyed reading this series on **The Myths of Fashion Design**.

## PART 3

# HUMOUR BEHIND THE SCENES

***Life is full of lessons... Many that I have learnt on the job, and ones which have made me laugh out loud...***

*The third part of this book takes you on a journey; one which is filled with laughter and joy, and with valuable lessons and insights these funny anecdotes has taught me...*

CHAPTER 3.1

# The 'Not Invented by Me' Syndrome

How many times have we witnessed good ideas go down the drain because someone in the system vociferously opposed it?

Too many to count, isn't it?

In my career, I have seen many such incidents, but one stays fresh in my mind...

This incident occurred a few years back.

A *Ms.Young* energetic buyer was recruited in our team to drive the sell throughs of a key but non-performing category. She brought a lot of new ideas with her, was enthusiastic about the category and took up rather unique initiatives.

2 months passed.

6 months passed.

12 months passed.

But nothing happened! Sales continued to stagnate.

One day, she came up to me, after a rather difficult Monday morning review. Distressed and irritated, she said,

*Graphic created by insideapparel.net

"*But what is the issue*?", I asked her!

"*Our competition is constantly innovating and introducing newness in the product range. This keeps them ahead of us*", she said.

She discussed how she had put together an innovation pipeline and worked with the fabric team, designers and vendors to come up with some new age products. She created marketable ideas, worked out the promotions and then presented it.

To her utter surprise, every one of her ideas went either into rework or were dropped.

This discussion stayed in my mind, thereafter. I kept pondering over why her ideas were dumped. One day, while interacting with her team leader, I understood what had happened.

Introducing *Mr. Team Leader.*

*Graphic created by insideapparel.net

He truly believed that he was a brilliant buyer and fancied himself to be an innovator par excellence. His arrogance made him overlook many unique initiatives by his team, many going waste, like our case in discussion. In fact, his team refrained from taking up such projects and eventually became 'Yes-Men'. The mere fact that a young buyer had taken the initiative to work on innovations did not go down well with him.

His logic was simple.

IF I DID NOT INVENT IT, IT'S NOT GOOD ENOUGH! and he genuinely believed in this.

*Ms.Young* energetic buyer eventually was recognised as a power house of talent and recruited by our competitors. *Mr. Team Leader* continues to be the same arrogant leader he always was…

This incident, though an everyday occurring, did teach me something!

- It's what I now call,

*Graphic created by insideapparel.net

We see good ideas biting the dust too often to count. Most of the times, it's because people don't want to listen. The team leaders come with the "Been there - Done that" attitudes and refuse to see the obvious. **The solutions are right there, staring us in our face, and yet our egos make us look the other way.** We just need to silence it to be able to listen/see, appreciate and recognise them.

**This is the bane of the fashion industry. It's so subjective that a little success can sometimes build big egos which become our blind spots. It slows down the team's efforts and creates a negative environment for all.**

In the end, I would only say that we should simply learn to open ourselves to listening, learning, and understanding everyone's inputs. All our stakeholders want us to succeed as in our success lies theirs too. All we must do is move beyond the '**NOT INVENTED BY ME**' syndrome.

CHAPTER 3.2

# Roughly Right or Perfectly Late???

"*Have no fear of perfection - you'll never reach it.*" So rightly said by Salvador Dali.

The word '**Perfection**' has been an enigma my whole life. We all want it, but is it what's needed?

This simple incident directed me towards an answer to this question.

A few years back, we were working on a new initiative to reduce our lead time and get to market quickly. There was a lot of pressure. *Mr. Sells Maximus* had joined us as the sales head, and he was trying to maximise business in his channel.

He had taken up the challenge of increasing his business manifold. He held multiple meetings with the channel partners, the design, product and sourcing teams. He even had meetings with the vendors to tie up all the loose ends.

His ask was very simple:

- A system which offers fast fashion to the channels
- React to the market in 8 weeks with the required product

SOP's were set up, regular reviews were planned, approval processes were defined and nothing was left to chance.

Or so he thought!

Everyone went into hyper drive. Work started in right earnest. Ball started rolling!

But he soon ran into an unusual problem.

The stakeholders seemed to be dealing with some commitment issues!

Yes, you heard that right.

They just would not commit an end date. And every time there was a review, there were new curve balls thrown in the form of open points.

By the 3rd week, it had become obvious that the timelines were derailed.

Costs were not getting closed, vendors were not committing to timelines, no closure on colours, so on and so forth…

He decided to roll up his sleeves and dive right into each issue. And to his utter surprise, he came face to face with his nemesis,

- Designer refused to delegate approvals to the vendor
- Product manager refused to close the cost till he got a detailed cost sheet
- Vendor refused to give a detailed cost as he wanted to vet every single variable like final fabric width, consumption etc.
- Mill refused to confirm the ex-mill date till griege was in-house
- Vendor refused to confirm a delivery date before he got a final date from the mill

Bottomline, there were no closures.

All exhausted, our hero came to me and asked a simple question.

*Graphic created by insideapparel.net

Frankly, I still do not have an answer for this!

He was clearly frustrated. But the other stakeholders could not see the problem.

They genuinely wanted to give him a 'correct' answer. And therein, lies the problem.

How much precision is required to conduct business? Is it better to be quick and roughly right rather than miss the bus in search of **PERFECTION**?

When companies have too many specialists and they lose sight of the final objective, they lose their nimbleness and speed. They focus on process and perfection rather than speed and the big picture.

Businesses need to develop a culture which balances out the above. The answer is always in the balance. In ancient Indian texts, there is a word for this - '*samay-achaar*', or simply put 'adapt your approach/style/process based on the need of the situation'.

CHAPTER 3.3

# The Quality of Errors!

‘**Quality**’ a word that everyone in the organisation is scared of, but passionate about…

What does it mean? No one knows.

It’s one of the most dynamic words used in the industry, solely defined by the stakeholder’s perception.

How this quality is understood by all is a mystery to most, a lesson I learnt in my first job.

It started one fine morning, when *Mr. Lead M. All*, our chairman, walked into the office fuming. He summoned every stakeholder to his room. This included the CEO, the merchandising head, the quality head, the product and design teams.

‘Oh! boy’, was it baptism by fire for us young trainees who had just joined the company.

**As we all filled into the room, we could only see two things:**

**One**, the anger on his face and

**Second**, the pile of three shirts on his desk…

And suddenly he looked at the quality head and roared.

*Graphic created by insideapparel.net

After a minute of silence, the quality head mustered the courage to ask,

"*But what happened*?"

"*See this*", said the chairman…

Unfolding the shirts one at a time, he pointed to the many issues. A loose button, faded colors, uncut threads and so on. With each issue, his voice got louder, and our heads hung lower. And then in an obviously foul mood, he said "*I don't even know why I've hired you guys!*"

We all slunk out of his room in utter dismay. Everyone huddled around *Mr. Qualithello*, the head of quality giving him questioning looks, "*Who's the auditor on this? How did he allow this to pass? Does he even know how to check?*"

"*But we did not come up with the instructions, we just executed them*", he muttered under his breath.

And then started the '*tandav*'.

*Graphic created by insideapparel.net

*Graphic created by insideapparel.net

*Graphic created by insideapparel.net

*Graphic created by insideapparel.net

In the meantime, the *Mr. Qualithello* had called the vendor in, who quietly heard us out and then asked for the garments in question. He inspected them and said,

"*These have all been made within specifications, all approvals are in place.*"

He then started showing us the detailed style file maintained by the factory.

Thus, the morning passed with everyone furious and playing the blame game with panache. Tired with the day's activities, and with no solution in sight, everyone decided to pass on the task to the kids in the system, namely us - The Trainees...

We were told to figure out the root cause of the problem. With no clue in hand, we turned to the chairman's secretary.

"*His friend picked up these pieces from our store and his driver handed them over in the morning*", she said.

So, in our innocence, we took the friend's phone number and called him up.

"*The garments have faded, the jeans have become loose and I was wondering if someone could get that button fixed*", he said. On further enquiry, we learnt that these garments had been purchased over **six months** back.

His friend was extremely happy that someone had spoken to him. We also had his clothes ironed and returned to him with the button fixed. His driver came and took the pieces.

In the evening, the chairman, beaming and obviously happy left for the day, breezing past us sharing general pleasantries.

This incident taught a valuable lesson.

Quality is defined by different stakeholders differently.

**For the customer**, it is fit, hand-feel, lustre, vibrancy of colour, whether the garment behaves well after multiple wears, no obvious defects like tears, stains etc.

**For the designer**, it has to be a perfect representation of what's been conceived in her/his mind. Is the colour matching perfectly, the fit is as per specification given, wash, hand-feel etc., as defined.

**For the product merchandising team**, it's about matching what the designer has defined, but with commercial tweaks gleaned from sales feedback.

**For the sourcing teams and vendors**, it's about matching expectations, but within cost and given timelines.

**It's the quality team**, that has the dirty job of auditing at various stages to ensure the products come out right.

In other words, most of what is understood as quality by the customer, is defined by design and product teams and the rest is just about whether those defined parameters have been met in production or not.

Unfortunately, it's the quality team that takes the brunt of the criticism, the only time someone remembers them is when something has gone wrong. When things go well, everyone else gets the credit. There is very little in quality team's hands,

- They do not make the specifications
- They don't select the vendor
- They don't close the costs

They just advise on technical issues and audit, but they are the ones who carry the can every time there is a customer return or complaint.

**Most companies do not even realise that a lot of customer complaints are unjustified and occur due to garment mishandling, post purchase. And the rest are mostly about fits and aesthetics on which the quality teams do not have a say. But every time the word quality comes up, everybody looks at the quality team for answers.**

This does not mean that they don't make mistakes. Sometimes they do, then improvement plans, and processes should be put in place. But most of our other stakeholders do not realise that a larger aspect of quality, as understood by the consumer, is about how the product has been defined.

So, the question I ask is – 'Who is responsible for quality? The guys who define or the guys who police?'

I feel, we need to approach quality more holistically in an integrated manner where all the stakeholders clearly understand and look at fulfilling consumer expectations rather than, their own narrow definitions of quality. Hence, the truth lies somewhere in between.

CHAPTER 3.4

# The Order of The Phoenix!

How often have we heard this dialogue from many buyers in office? They keep resurrecting with order emails every now & then…

**But is an email or a phone call an order?**

Let me share a humorous incident from my first job which answers this question.

Straight out of traineeship, I was moved into the merchandising at this company which was a pioneer of sorts in our country. It was a fashion retail chain with stores across the country and many private labels along with a few brands.

The company was growing at an unprecedented rate and almost doubling in size every year. But the supply chain can be at best defined as erratic. Being managed by the many different private label teams, it was confusing and chaotic.

The Chairman, *Mr. Allead Dumbledore,* had decided in his wisdom that it was time to professionalise the sourcing function and got *Mr. Sourcerers Stone* to join the team as the sourcing head. He was tasked with standardising the processes, setting up SOP's, conducting regular reviews etc.

In his quest to be known as fair and sincere, he started pushing us for clear data, quick closures and details. This did not go down very well with my boss *Ms. Merchandising Myrtle*, the Buying and Merchandising head. She was a spitfire, best described by the Hindi word *'Dabang'*, meaning brazen, daring, direct…

And so, a few months into his new role, *Mr. Sourcerers Stone* was summoned to the Chairman's office. On entering, he was ushered into the conference room, where he was ambushed by our *'Dabang'* leader and us.

After being chastised on some of the trailing deliveries, our *Dabang* leader got to the point.

*Graphic created by insideapparel.net

*Graphic created by insideapparel.net

"*See! This is what I am saying? Your team has not even placed the order. You are not even aware*"? *Dabang* was in full flow. She had the sourcing head where she wanted him - on the run.

"*Let me call my team lead for this category*"', *Mr. Sourcerers Stone* said in distress.

"Have we got a blazer order from them", he asked his team lead when he came in.

"*Yes, sir*", said the team lead cautiously, not knowing what he had walked into.

"*Why did this order not reflect in the ORM (Operational Review Meeting, for the ignoramus) data when we reviewed it yesterday*", he was asked.

"*Oh! That's because I received an* **enquiry** *on mail from their buyer yesterday asking if it was possible to make blazers in six weeks and supply for Diwali. They have an enquiry from one of their channels*"', the man was visibly relaxed, now that he knew what the issue was. "*And I have already called for swatches for selection from available stock*". There was stunned silence in the room.

To the chairman, the issue was being built around the incompetence of the sourcing team and their new head. How did he not even know that there was an order on hand?!

*Mr. Allead Dumbledore*, who obviously was a past master at dealing with such situations, quickly seized the opportunity to make a point.

"*For it to be construed an order, it has to have all specifications clearly defined and documented. What is the fabric code, BOM, fit specifications? Without such clear definition, it cannot be an order, it's an enquiry. It is the business team's responsibility to ensure that sufficient details are provided to the sourcing team, enabling them to process an order*".

Turning to us he said that "*there is a difference between an '**order**' and an '**enquiry**' or '**intent**'. It actually takes a lot of work to issue an order*".

And then to *Mr. Sourcerous Stone*, "*Put together a minimum threshold, below which you will not consider it a live order, at least 4 or 5 mandatory fields in an order form*".

There are many lessons in this anecdote – definitely, behavioural and management lessons, but what the chairman then sat and defined was pertinent and relevant in all situations.

## 'Enquiry' or 'Intent to Order' is not an Order

Orders are clear liabilities which the business is undertaking, hence they must be in black and white.

For orders to be actionable, they must mandatorily contain sufficient information to process.

What's the big deal with this? It's common sense, you will say.

Well, strangely enough, it's not! This is the bane of the fashion industry. It's a highly subjective industry and extremely people-dependent. How well-made or how fast your goods come in is decided more by how well the order is defined and how clearly all the data is given.

CHAPTER 3.5

# Different Quality for Different Folks

Isn't it surprising how we all tend to see every situation with the same glasses on? We apply the same standards and measure everything against the same yardstick. We apply a 'one size fits all' policy…

But why?

In the quest to find an answer to that question, I started thinking about an incident that occurred while I was still at my first job. It was the late 80's/ early 90's. The retail industry had started growing at a fast pace and business was booming.

But then came the **1st disruption** in the business!

A formal shirt brand called Stencil. Tapping in the value segment, they launched cotton formal shirts for Rs.199.

Yes, you read that right… Rs.199 it was. It was quite the rage and had taken the market by storm.

So, *Mr. Lead M. All*, our chairman, had a quick meeting with my boss *Ms. Buying Beauty*.

*Graphic created by insideapparel.net

Such projects were nothing new for my boss. She was used to these reactionary projects from the chairman, every time he came across anything new. And many a times, he even forgot some of these projects. But every time he came up with these ideas, they used to create quite the stir in the office.

So, not realising the importance of one more new project, this was passed on to me.

*Graphic created by insideapparel.net

And so began my indoctrination into product development.

I went from team to team to figure out how to get that product right. Unfortunately, success seemed like an elusive dream to me.

From the designer to the fabric team, from the trims to the tech team, everyone told me the same thing – *"We are doing the best in the given quality"*.

A week passed by without any progress.

Then came that day when the chairman wanted to know what was taking so much time?

My boss, sitting right beside me, was equally baffled by the outcome of this exercise. Cost re-engineering was still not a developed skill set in the company.

And then began a masterclass by the **Big Bad Wolf** himself. A lesson that has stayed with me ever since.

*Graphic created by insideapparel.net

"*Let's take away the box pleat at the back. Can we reduce the length by an inch? What about the matching parameters? Do we need matching shoulder, sleeve, cuff, cuff placket? What about the cut and sew placket, do we need it?*" And he then went on to discuss every trim used, thread quality, packing material and, lo and behold, in 20 minutes, we had cracked the entry price point of the shirt.

But my boss was still not convinced, "*This is not what our customers expect in terms of quality*", she held her ground.

"*Do you know the difference between the German cars and the others?*" He asked, alluding to his prized Mercedes, which in those days was a rarity in the country.

"*Do you think the quality expectation is the same for these and the others which are one tenth the cost?*"

"*Quality is how you define the specifications. The important thing is - is the consumer accepting it happily?*"

He asked us to do a small test market for these in two of our flagship stores in Delhi.

The rest, as they say, is history. Our new price point product did well for some time, as did that new brand. But as it happens often, in this graveyard of fashion brands, both have been relegated to the annals of the Indian Fashion Industry history.

Quality is how you define the product specification. Different customer sets have different expectations of quality at different prices.

Therefore, it's different quality for different folks.

You may think this is simple and everyone understands it. Well, truth be told, most companies struggle with the concept of defining quality differently for different price points and products. They get used to following the same standards for everything in the company which leads to higher costs and longer lead times, just to name a few issues.

CHAPTER 3.6

# Decoding the Consumer Code

Do the consumers care about the count of the fabric?

Do they walk into the store and get enthralled by the season's concept/story?

Do they care that this 'Red' is not 'The Red'?

What does the consumer really see? A piece of art or a practical clothing?

The answer to this question has partly been a mystery to me. And every time I think about this, I am reminded of a rather weird incident which took place early in my career.

My first job was with a company, best described as one of the pioneers of fashion retail in India. They had a chain of retail stores across the country, through which they retailed a variety of private labels and brands.

I had the privilege of being part of the first batch of management trainees they had hired. And they had such grandiose plans for us. A stint in the stores, then factory, followed by the warehouse and finally moving into buying and merchandising.

But as often happens with the best laid plans of man, it went awry the moment we reported in the stores.

*Graphic created by insideapparel.net

Yes, the sales team quit! And we had no choice but to fill in. So, here we were, 4 management trainees in that store, trying our best to figure out how to manage our counters. Sales obviously went down as the whole sales team had quit en masse. *Mr. GM Manageus*, the general manager in utter desperation, decided that we needed training.

And who better than the design and buying teams to train us novices.

So, in they strutted, and we spent two hours every day being taken through the whole product line.

We were given the complete encyclopedia. From yarn, to dying, fabric, trims, stitching, fits, construction, benefits, styling details, it was enormous. Then we were told about how lines are conceptualised, designs created, samples made and then produced, wow! It was like rocket science to us young kids.

We never realised that so much went into clothes.

Armed with all this amazing knowledge and new-found confidence, we decided to attack our sales targets with renewed vigour.

*Graphic created by insideapparel.net

But lo and behold! The consumer taught us a very different lesson. Most of what we had learnt did not actually help us. What the consumer wanted was very different.

But something else hit me like a ton of bricks!!

*Graphic created by insideapparel.net

When a consumer walks into the store, he/she sees hundreds of garments at one glance. Only 1-2 garments may attract their attention, while the rest are lost in this abyss.

What takes the teams 6 months of hard work, conceptualisation, trials, sourcing and manufacturing does not even attract the consumers' attention for a fraction of a second. The consumer doesn't even spend a moment before rejecting it.

I realised that the most important aspect of business is to understand what grabs the consumers' attention and why a product is successful in doing so. Unfortunately, this is usually the most neglected aspect in our industry.

I figured that we need to simplify the way we design.

- We need to understand and work on what grabs the consumers' attention
- The product benefit is conveyed using simple messaging
- Keeping innovations relevant to the consumers is key

Anything else we do is pointless and a wasted effort.

I then developed a habit that has stayed with me through the years.

*Graphic created by insideapparel.net

This has given me a unique perspective and helped me in my work, throughout my career.

My friends, who I take shopping, ask such questions through their innocence and simplicity that can disarm the most potent designer or buyer.

Many a times, in fact most of the times, we obsess and work on so many things, most of which the consumer does not even notice.

My advice is to see and think like the customer and things may just start looking very different.

CHAPTER 3.7

# The Vanity of Sizes

What size do you wear?

Often, the answer to that question is '**Hesitation**'.

Yes, you read that right. Hesitation it is!

In a world where body-shaming is still a reality, opening up about the size of your clothes or your preferred fits is a very difficult thing to do. Particularly, when you walk into a store and ask the salesperson for your size.

This is not just because of how the outside world judges you, but it's also a matter of self-perception.

Of course, these things don't matter if you have spent hours working out and have a body you can flaunt (and these people are rare).

What does that have to do with fashion retail, you say?

Well! A lot.

Particularly, if you are selling in a store.

My last chapter rejigged my memory and reminded me of many incidents from my first job. Some from days I spent on the retail floor which gave me insights into the consumers' minds.

For those who came in late. As management trainees, we were sent to the store for some months to sell, but we ended up managing the whole counter ourselves.

So, there I was in my first job, trying my best to manage my sales targets.

**And these were the days when no one taught you much.**

**We just learnt on the job. And the consumers taught me a lesson I cherish till date.**

One of those days, in walked a customer and

Not to offend her, I quietly gave her the piece in a size 28 to try.

And a few minutes later, with irritation written large all over her face, she said "*your fit is bad, I don't like it*".

'But . . but . .'

Before I could say much, she had already turned around and left.

Another day, another customer, similar story ...

He had wanted to try our new Italian slim fit, but he had heavy thighs, and it did not fit him well.

I soon realised that:

- I was spending too much time doing re-trials and losing other customers in that time
- Customers always had a slimmer image of themselves in their heads
- They did not know what type of fit worked for them
- They quickly lost interest, if the first trial did not work. Convincing them to try another fit, would lose me 60% of the other customers

So, after another bad week of sales, I got down to some serious thinking. How do I overcome this problem? And then suddenly...

I figured out a simple formula. And it took me some time to learn this, but learn I did.

- Guess the customer's size correctly before asking him
- Anticipate which body type he is and understand which fit would work best for him
- So, after asking him his preference, I would always slip in an extra piece which I knew would work, and quietly request him to try that as well.

And lo and behold! My first trial hit rate improved, so did my sales because I could attend to more customers and convert more trials into sales.

While this is an old anecdote (the late '80s) and retailing has since evolved – the basics have remained the same.

Conversion rate, communication of fit, and body types continue to be as relevant today as always.

**In fact, communication of fit is of the utmost importance in today's digital age, where a consumer does not interact with a salesperson. He/She buys the product based on what's communicated on the web page.**

Good understanding of consumers' approach to sizing and communication of sizes and fits, lead to lesser returns, fewer dissatisfied consumers and forming of better brand perception amongst the consumers.

Many brands have institutionalised vanity sizing and changed their fits and sizes to ensure that they flatter the customers' ego.

Anticipation and understanding the customers' requirement and ensuring that you give them what works for them, and by understanding their requirement better than them, remains the key to higher conversion and earning their trust.

CHAPTER 3.8

# Grab that Attention

Let me ask you a question…

What do you think is the scarcest resource in the world?

Yes, my friends, it is '**Attention**'.

And why is attention scarce?

Because it is so difficult to grab.

What happens when we walk into a store? Or open an e-commerce webpage? Or any of the social media accounts?

We are bombarded with information - each trying to grasp our attention. Every inch of our view is branded with messages, colour, music, smell and design fighting for our attention.

What do you think this does to our attention? **It fragments it, makes it jumpy and that results in a very small attention span**. We become much like 'grasshoppers', fluttering from one place to another.

Studies show that the **average human being now has an attention span of 8 seconds**. This is a sharp decrease from the average attention span of 12 seconds in the year 2000. More shocking, perhaps, is the fact that research has found that human attention span decreases by a whopping 88% every year.

Take a minute to soak that in as I recount yet another incident from my early days in retail.

For those who came in late, as a management trainee, I was sent to the store for some months to sell but I ended up managing the whole counter as all the sales staff quit. So, there I was in my first job, trying my best to manage my sales targets.

Now, try as I might, the sales targets were always elusive. There was a lot of pressure from HO to meet our targets. Even the Chairman made a few visits to see how things were going.

It is here that I had a revelation. **Customers (and people in general) have very short attention spans.**

By the time you explain them one thing, they have moved onto to the 10th.

One of those days, in walked a customer who demonstrated this to me.

'Well. ..' I gave him an explanation on how the newly introduced trouser was a superior product. Thank God! I remembered some of the product training.

"*Do you have it in my size?*"

"*Let me check?*" I said, and quickly checked the pile on the shelf for the piece, which was not there. "*I think it's in the storeroom, I will just be back*".

I went quickly to the store and rummaged through the stocks and there it was at the bottom of the pile. With a sense of great achievement, I rushed back.

But where was the customer?

I looked left, looked right. The customer had vanished.

There was this empty feeling in the pit of my stomach. Had I taken too long?

I looked at my watch - 6 minutes – oh! It's okay! I thought . . .

I started walking through the store to see if the customer was still there. And there he was, in another section, looking at the products.

He looked blankly at me when I offered him his size. "*Ah! Yes*", he remembered. And politely took the piece to the trial room. "*This fit is fine*", he said coming out, "*Do you have that dark grey colour in this? I think I like that colour more*".

On the inside, I was dismayed as I could see another customer in my section who was going unattended.

With a polite smile, I said "*Of course, just give me a minute. I will get it for you*".

I had no idea if I had that piece in stock. It would take me another 6 minutes to get the size. In the meanwhile, I would probably lose the customer browsing in my section. But I would at least get this sale.

Unfortunately, by the time I came back with the piece, the customer had left. And I lost that sale. Not just one, but two.

And then I started seeing a pattern. I realized, there were quite a few cases like this. I thought maybe if I could not waste time while attending to customers, it would allow me to multi-attend and close sale faster.

And then I came up with a **3-Step Formula** to help myself.

- The product posters & tags helped me in explaining the product to the customer while allowing me to multi-attend other customers.
- The cheat sheet was a pencil written inventory which always stayed in my pocket. I would cross off pieces sold and add pieces which came in. At any point I knew what my inventory was.
- In the store, I made a system of keeping inventory in a way that I knew exactly where the pieces were.

I did feel a lot more confident after this and it helped improve my hit rate.

But the lesson I learnt was that consumers have a very short attention span. And if **you have not hooked them in that span or ensured that they find it easy to shop and try, either you have lost the sale or lost a future sale.**

While retail has truly evolved in these many years and so much is done by artificial intelligence, systems, store talkers, marketing material etc., yet the fact remains simple.

- Keep your communication simple and clear
- If it's important then that communication bears repeating
- Do not waste the consumers' time if you do not know the answer to a question
- Anticipate, plan and keep the consumer engaged

Whether you are in retail or online, these principles remain the same.

CHAPTER 3.9

# From the Readers' Mind!

It was late one evening when Anindya gave me a call to discuss a new idea for the chapter. With excitement in his voice, he said,

Joining his excitement, I said "*Do you want to add quirk & a little bit of humour to these stories?*" Should we keep the narrative simple and personalised...? and so the discussion continued.

After some time, the next set of chapters started taking shape in our minds... And what followed was a series relating '8 incidents' from Anindya's life which have not just taught him something, but also taught the readers many things.

As always, our readers have joined in with enthusiasm and shared many valuable comments. We thank you all, whole heartedly, for extending this support and truly **making Inside Apparel a platform for everyone's expression.**

Some of the comments are shared in this article. Enjoy!

## NURTURE AND EMPOWER

*"A qualified younger talent in your team (who has been put together, by adopting professional recruiting methods, with the team leader as an integral part) will only yield desired results if the team is empowered enough.*

*Nurturing and promoting them leads to a very conducive environment for generating newer concepts & innovative ideas.*

*Insecurity will never blind an open and delegating leader as it ultimately ups his/her rank and image.*

*At the end, it's the product not personalities that's going to drive the market".*

- Paresh Shah

## INCENTIVISE RISK TAKING

*"This is relevant for all companies. Innovation is a risk-taking venture. Companies by design are structured to mitigate risk. I personally don't think it's a problem of the Mr. Team Leader alone. How do companies incentivise risk-taking and encourage it (within limits)? Creating a 'safe space' for risk taking is important. One suggestion could be to set aside a certain % of innovative styles to be created and then see what the results are".*

- Gunish Jain (CEO BlueKaktus)

## CHANGE IN ORGANISATIONAL CULTURE

*"This is so true. But how to address such issues is also very important. The company, as a whole, should have a mechanism to check and resolve. Otherwise,*

*the company loses all the talent to competitors and will struggle to grow, and eventually fail, even with 'know it all' team leads. What if these team leads never realise their shortcomings? What if there is no one to bell the cat? I would like to know your opinion on that."*

- Prasenjit Adhikari, Creative Director Arrow @ Arvind brands

## PERFECTION IS GOOD TO IDEALISE

*"In a real situation, you have to keep an eye on a multitude of factors and take calls, accordingly.*

*These things make me wonder – Does Perfection exist? Like beauty, 'perfection lies in the eyes of beholder'. To what scale you want to bend down to ensure it's PERFECT. Commercial calls and conditional approvals are taken to avoid such situation – but do we mine that data – the winner/losers out of the calls taken and learn to bend our curve of perfection, to get to the path of winning the situation - keeping in mind the past mistakes".*

- Sarika Arora, Head Corporate Sales at Royal Data Matics Pvt. Ltd.

## THE PANDEMIC HAS MADE THINGS HAPPEN

*"This year, we have for the first time moved from top-down approach to a collaborative approach and have been successful in reducing delivery lead time, and the collaborative creativity took efficiency to another level. Delivery in 45 days in India!*

*Colour approval digitally and closing styles over zoom calls.*

*It has been a rush and if we collaborate at design and buyer level with production and factory at one time, we will reduce 50% of the timeline.*

*This is with caution - it's the smart working between the brands and the factory supply from mills, there has seen no change, but the process time reduced with the transfer of responsibility to the factory for yarn colour approvals and flexibility in the approach".*

- Akhil Khanna, Managing Director, SRV Knittech Pvt Limited

## QUALITY AS IT SHOULD BE

*"The prime job of any quality person or head is the ability to predict and forecast errors. He must consolidate the requirements of designer, brand value, vendor capabilities, sourcing requirements. Every product has a CTQ (critical to quality). Inspections are again classified as Predictive, Preventive and Detection. If all three fail, without any documentation, it's quality team's responsibility. This defines how good our processes are. The final check*

*between the design/development/procurement/manufacture is the audits before it reaches customer".*

- Ajay Ravuri, General Manager, Quality, Arvind Fashions Limited

## COST OF POOR QUALITY

*"Once the COST of poor quality is clearly understood across the cross functions and driven top down, the probability of everyone smiling is higher, if not - it will remain a B-Lame game".*

- Sandeep Golam, Director operations, Denimach Limited

## ORDER PLACEMENT IS A FINANCIAL LIABILITY

*"This is a typical situation in our industry. Orders are placed without details. Sometimes due to ignorance, at other times due to assumptions. To solve this issue, a good sourcing head always makes some fields mandatory for an order to exist. An order is also a financial liability to a company, so in many companies the finance guys are also involved for second level, for an order to exist. Typically, an order should be raised on the system by the buyer. Level 1 approval should be the junior sourcing merchant who has to execute the order. Level 2 should be Finance to accept the finances are allocated and level 3 should be the sourcing head to accept the order for the team to execute. If this basic procedure is followed by companies, there will never be a slip in the system".*

- Poonam Sood Lal, Consultant, Co-Founder Sash Exports (Buying House)

## TECHNOLOGY TO THE RESCUE

*"I like the humour intertwined with a critical message. This reminds me of a placard on the desk of the sourcing head of an apparel company. It reads as - "In this place everyone wants stuff delivered yesterday. If you want something today, then come tomorrow." Jokes apart, the situation described was commonplace, but hopefully with the advent of the systems, things have gotten better".*

- Krishna Kumar (KK), IT Entrepreneur and Supply Chain Enthusiast

## HOW THINGS WORK TODAY

*"This was then, what is the scenario now - with so many brands of various scale, with 35% of consumption of garments happening on a platform that doesn't allow customer to feel much at the time of purchase but views quality post purchase, in the convenience of his or her home. The expectation of today's customer, even if*

*she buys disposable fast fashion product or a well curated product, is almost the same. Why do brands have to then focus on educating the customer about the quality standards and how one thing is better than the other. Millions are spent to tell the quality story through various mediums - does the customer really know or want the given quality ever? It sometimes makes me wonder what the basic hygiene in quality is and how much extra do brands put and then educate and charge thousands extra".*

- Himanshu Singh, Co-founder, Meraki

## WHAT ABOUT BRAND VALUE

*"This will help to get some business immediately but where is brand value? If one brand is setting different quality level with different price range, especially in apparel sector, I think it will affect brand value in the long run".*

- Dipin KK

## CUSTOMER CENTRICITY IS KEY TO SUCCESS

*"We live in interesting digital times where customer choices are driven by known and unknown influencers and influences. Going forward, technology will have to deduce what you simply observed in buying behaviour. The principle remains the same though!"*

- Nithya Easwaran, Managing Director, Multiples Alternate Asset Management Pvt Ltd

## OFFER SOLUTIONS TO CUSTOMERS

*"What you shared can be applied actually in every industry and domain. Your ability, to gauge and manage what your customer is thinking and offering solutions that will not make him uncomfortable for whatever reason, can be a great skill that all of us should learn".*

- Yogesh Agiwal, Founder & CEO, Crossover Leadership Journeys

## AN EXPERIENCE

*"I can totally relate to this article. I once went to a store and asked the salesperson to get me a waist size 32 jeans, and he said that as per him I should try 34. I told him, 'Do you know my waist better than I do!!!' and walked off. The next store I went – I told them that I wear size 34 and it fit!!!"*

- Gunish Jain, CEO BlueKaktus

## COMMUNICATION IS KEY

*"Communicating with the customer will reveal his quest for a fit preference, while gauging the size should be learnt while indulging in a conversation.*

*And not to say the knowledge about the product on the floor is vital. This is so because same size is a different size for each brand. What size 36 could be for one brand will be different for another brand".*

- Sanjay Lal, Co-founder, Sash Exports (Buying House)

## What You Sow Is What You Reap

*"Many many many times, I have walked into branded stores and for more than a few minutes no one ever came near me. All the store staff, including the store manager, are busy with their own thing when there is no other customer except me. They all see me in the store. But ... the store manager is super busy with his computer. The store staff are chatting about the movie they saw or some gossip.*

*Every time I have walked out .... the worst is when no one has even asked me why I am leaving or what am I looking for. In most cases, I have gone with clear intention of a specific purchase. This has happened in the last 20 years, hundreds of times, specifically with branded stores in malls as well as high streets. Sometimes, I have even shouted at them about their attitude and have told them that they are killing the brand.*

*But the most interesting thing is .... I have seen this happening to me far less in small multi-brand stores run by owners. There someone will come to me within 90 seconds of me walking into the store, asking me "Sir, what do you want?' or 'Sir, Can I help you?'.*

*So, you can understand when many single-branded stores owned by the companies do less sales ... RMKV, Nallis, Kumaran, Chennai Sillks doing roaring sales even during the pandemic time. One of the biggest lessons I learnt was from my father, a second-class educated, retailer of stores: 'Greet the customers within 30 seconds of entry and ensure someone is there to attend to them (This used to be a shop where we had counters between the product and the customer) & ensure no customer is unattended even if it is about managing more than three customer families, at a time, during seasons.*

*What came to me is a simple principle – 'You have to give attention if you want to grab anyone's attention'.*

*This leads to a very simple fundamental principle of life: 'What you give is what you get back from the world'.*

*I remembered a Tamil quote that I read in early childhood: "வினை விதைத்தவன் வினை அறுப்பான், தினை விதைத்தவன் தினை அறுப்பான்."*

*It means: 'You reap what you sow'."*

- Raja Chidambaram

These anecdotes have reflected on many facets of our industry. From the leaders to the consumers, from communication to attention…

Each anecdote shared has opened our eyes to multitude learnings and given us something to think about. It's always good to learn from others' experiences for they are the mistakes you avoid and learnings you gain.

# PART 4

# WHAT IS THE SECRET SAUCE OF CREATING EFFICIENT SUPPLY CHAINS?

***Rarely people understand the importance of supply chain for it is the pillar on which this industry stands.***

Supply chain efficiency is of utmost importance when we look at the fashion industry. Failing at creating an efficient supply chain would mean failing in creating a sustainable business. The part 4 of this book dwells into some of the secrets which I have learnt, over time, in this industry.

CHAPTER 4.1

# Trust-Based Supply Chains

## 4 Principles for Building Trust in Supply Chain

The apparel industry came into existence from the time humans learnt how to make clothes. It has grown over centuries and has become a powerhouse, which drives consumer behaviour across the world.

However, for an industry this old, it comes across as a rather fragmented one. The supply chain is of particular concern in an industry with a few large players and none being dominant (size or scale).

Time & again, I have noticed that the unorganised sector works faster and more efficiently when compared to the organised sector. The key reason which drives this difference is **"TRUST"**.

## "TRUST CREATES A SEAMLESS SUPPLY CHAIN IN THE UNORGANISED INDUSTRY"

From cotton to yarn, to fabric, to trims, everyone works on trust in the unorganised sector. This trust is built over many years of working, and one is seamlessly able to meet expectations fashioning a smooth supply chain. Even today, your '*Zubaan*' (spoken word) is your bond in Mumbai's Wholesale Textile Market.

This is possible because, in the unorganised sector, business owners transact directly with each other. However, due to scale and corporatisation, the organised sector no longer enjoys the benefit of such trust.

In developed markets like the USA, contracts form the basis of a working relationship. Inevitably, these contracts are one sided and tend to favour the larger entity which strains the relationships further. Hence, vendors and buyers tend to find comfort in operational level relationships, which often change with the employees. New partnerships are formed as new employees move.

The buzzword in the industry today is '**Agile Supply Chain**', but the question I ask is more fundamental. Can there be agility without trust? Trust between vendors and businesses lead to a bond akin to partnership, each going the extra mile for the other. This leads to a 'Seamless Supply Chain', going well past the definition of agile.

While everyone is discussing the future of supply chain, in the post COVID era, it would be good to remember these simple fundamentals as they will continue to drive business relationships irrespective of how the world may change. In fact, building trust, in a time of great uncertainty, will probably be the difference between a good and a great supply chain.

So, how does one go about building trust?

## Having studied this over the past few years, I have battled for building trust in the organised sector, with a set of 4 principles:

### 1. Build a Culture Based on Ethics

Businesses need to create a culture, within their own teams, which allow honest evaluation of issues and not cover up by shifting blame. Hence, a combination of the brand/retailer's manufacturing terms, and management decisions influence how its representatives (namely buyers/merchants) identify and adjudicate issues. Their judgements are then based on an honest assessment of the mistakes committed by either side.

Being ethical, honest and thorough will go a long way that can do wonders for relationships between vendors and customers. Moral reputation makes it easier to build trust, which is then difficult to break. Being honest and thorough also helps solve problems quicker with vendors.

Brands/retailers can exacerbate time pressures with poor forecasting, delays in providing necessary order specifications or approvals and sudden changes to order volumes, throwing off a factory's ability to plan. Businesses that take fair responsibility for delays, caused by their own teams, including those that allow flexible delivery schedules, pay for air freight to transport products faster or waive financial penalties.

Hence, a symbiotic relationship needs to be formed between both parties based on the mantra of **DEPENDABLE, CONSISTENT, TRANSPARENT & FLEXIBLE** combined with the principle of **4C's**. There must be an effort to institutionalise and sustain this in current practices.

## 2. Money Makes the World Go Round

Businesses need to plan their volumes and inward schedules, meticulously to ensure that their own inventory levels and cash cycles are healthy. They need to build processes that allow for flexibility in the supply chain without disrupting it. This will be discussed in greater detail in upcoming chapters. Companies also need to have a dedicated team in finance which works on giving financial solutions and predictability on cash flows to the vendors.

It's important to realise that timely payments are crucial. It is the key to retaining and adding good suppliers. Making sure that they are paid on time will prove that the brands/retailers are reliable customers and easy to work with. If for any reason customers cannot make the payments on an agreed date, then informing the supplier of a revised date, at the earliest, is also very important.

The payment chain or '**Vitamin-M**', as it's sometimes called, is very critical in business. A lot of the supplier base is in the MSME sector and extremely dependent on timely payments for their cash cycle.

## 3. Consistency Is the Key

Businesses need to have a well-articulated policy on vendor management with clearly demonstrated decision-making at the top to ensure that consistency is maintained at operational levels.

Vendors appreciate consistency of actions, decisions and behaviour in their relationships with the customer. While there may be short term blips, if the long-term trend is consistent, then the relationship will thrive. No vendor likes an over opportunistic customer.

It's also important to make sure you treat them well and don't neglect them. It is good to remember that your supplier isn't just working for your brand. Many may be supplying to your competitors. This type of understanding will benefit the relationship and motivate suppliers to spend more time working with your brand.

## 4. Collaboration Is the Only Way

A business functions well when everyone works together for better costs and higher margins, tackling each other's issues as their own. Buyers and vendors need to look at building a long-term relationship and not merely a transactional one. This helps both parties to achieve their goals and build long-term trust.

There must be a clear mechanism to set joint goals and measure achievements through a rigorous review process. This means institutionalising reviews, recognitions and celebrations. It is also important to ensure that vendors feel included in the success and growth of the company.

Changing business dynamics are a constant these days. In such a scenario, building a high trust environment between buyers and vendors leads to greater flexibility. Implementing new strategies, getting vendors to invest in new technologies, new innovations, going the extra mile for each other becomes increasingly easier if the relationship is based on trust.

A support system between vendor and brand may extend to jointly negotiating raw materials, holding inventory, blocking capacities, improving efficiencies and financials; primarily doing things which one would consider simply beyond transactional.

**TRUST-BASED SUPPLY CHAINS ARE THE FUTURE. THEY ARE THE MOST EFFICIENT & FLEXIBLE SUPPLY CHAINS, MAKING THEM AGILE & INNOVATIVE.**

CHAPTER 4.2

# Vendor-To-Vendor Partner

Over the years in the apparel industry, I have found that many vendors aspire to work with big brands and retailers. While they are able to procure orders for a season or two, they are unable to impress the brand/retailer teams to do long term business with them.

Reflecting on my experiences, I believe businesses are not just looking at capabilities and manufacturing infrastructure or cost, they desire qualities that will set the vendors apart from the rest, qualities that elevate them to another level in their eyes.

What are these desired qualities, brands/retailers look for in a preferred vendor partner?

The first desired quality in a vendor is being '**Dependable**'.

Brands/retailers prefer to work with vendors who can meet their COMMITMENTS on time, within cost parameters and requisite quality. Commitments that vendors successfully meet are then used to improve their own visibility which also reassures their customers of their dependability. This is commonly practiced by successful vendor partners.

The second desired quality in a vendor is being '**Consistent**'.

'**Every time, on time**', is a mantra every vendor needs to follow. Being dependable, every time, on delivery, quality and cost. Best in class vendors tend to formally brief their customers about this regularly, thus building their reputation for consistency. This builds trust and reliability that helps build a long-term business association, season after season.

The third desired quality in a vendor is being '**Transparent**'.

Transparency is the key to building trust in business. When vendors are transparent with respect to costing, social & legal compliance, as well as dealings with nominated vendors, businesses feel confident working with them. Another thing which is expected of vendors is transparency in declaring their daily/weekly status on orders which can be a major hinderance in building trust if not handled transparently.

The final desired quality in a vendor is being '**Flexible**'.

Business is dynamic in nature, and these days even more so. Support from the vendor becomes the need of the hour in many circumstances. This support may vary from holding the goods for an extended period to reprioritising for early deliveries, reworking commercial terms, changes in shipping instructions etc. By extending this support and being flexible, the vendor reassures the customer and builds trust which allows the brand/retailer to see the vendor as a partner as opposed to a transactional profiteer.

Over the years, I have seen that vendors display some of these qualities, but not all. Typically, they tend to build relationships with junior merchants or managers – but not the company. As a result, when these people move to other companies – so do the vendors.

**DEPENDABLE, CONSISTENT, TRANSPARENT & FLEXIBLE are not just words, they are mantras for each vendor to follow.**

A mantra which will make them a preferred partner with the brand/retailer. A mantra which makes businesses succeed.

Vendors, who can deliver these qualities, consistently earn the trust of the brand/retailer and become the preferred vendor partner. They become their 'go-to guides' for all things business.

**A mantra for all vendors to follow.**

CHAPTER 4.3

# How To Become A Preferred Customer?

We elaborated the qualities of a vendor partner in the previous article. While we look for these qualities in the vendor, we must keep in mind that trust works both ways.

Brands and retailers also need to ensure that they are **dependable** with their commitments, **consistent** with policies, **transparent** in their transactions and **flexible** in accommodating their vendor partner's needs in an ever-changing world.

We all know that vendors like regular confirmed orders, higher volumes, better prices or volume projections, to plan production.

However, the **real fulcrum** of the relationship with any vendor is built and maintained at the operational level.

One of pillars in the apparel industry is the **Buyer/Merchandiser**, and he/she is the key operational connect on a daily basis and is also empowered to take decisions that can make or break the end-to-end supply chain. This means that if brands/retailers wish to ensure trust, they must have a clear mechanism to manage the relationship at the ground level.

While we, time and again, speak about the expectations from the vendors, we tend to forget that it's a two-way street. Vendors also have expectations. After all, buyers are the channels for their businesses to grow. If the buyer/merchant can successfully gain the trust of the vendor, it would lead to the seamless functioning of the overall supply chain.

The buyer/merchant, while working at the operational level, manages most of the key levers that impact ease of doing business and efficiencies for the vendor. In my experience, this tends to define how the relationship works. So, how does the buyer gain the vendor's trust?

The **4C's which will make a buyer a preferred buyer** are:

**Clarity:** Communication is the key to a smooth supply chain. Lack of clarity plagues the apparel industry's backend. From dockets, to packing, to shipping instructions, to commercial terms, a buyer/merchant should ensure that all minute details are clear to the vendor. Approvals, at every stage of the development and manufacturing process, are the bane of the vendor existence and lack of clarity here leads to delays, conflicts, biases and mistrust.

Time and again, vendors receive ambiguous comments like 'sleeve needs to be longer', with no clarity on precise measurements or from where to where. This leads to many misunderstandings and delays. Clear communication should be taught and practised to ensure ease of business.

**Closure:** Quick decision-making i.e., closure helps ensure that all open points are closed quickly. A buyer should be empowered and prepared to take quick decisions and give closure on all issues, in the day-to-day functioning of the business - be it cost closure or approvals. This is one of the biggest pain points with vendors. We often have scenarios where the owner of a multi-million-dollar company is personally following up with a junior merchant in the retail/brand company because his work has come to a standstill due to non-closure of open items in the order.

Companies should ensure that strict TATs (Turn Around Time) are defined for approvals and cost closures, failing which there should be a well-oiled escalation matrix to support this. Buyers and merchants, when on leave or travelling, should ensure that they empower either someone else in the company or the vendor to close unresolved issues on approvals and costs.

Since, some of these approvals within the company are cross-functional i.e., handled by different teams within the same company, responsibilities tend to get lost in corporate hierarchy. This can easily be managed today using digital platforms which allow cross-functional workflows.

**Comfort:** Vendors should feel comfortable in reaching out to anyone in the organisation, be it other departments or the senior management. In case of any escalations, they should not fear a backlash from the team dealing with them, operationally. It's important that the buyers/merchandisers create a relationship based on trust rather than power.

The vendors' comfort also increases when they know that their customers have long term plans for them. Formal and regular reviews, to discuss performance and future plans with the vendors, and involving other departments in these meetings, make vendors feel included in the company. This is a tool that the buyer/merchant can use to gain trust and make them comfortable. Efforts should be made to make the vendor feel like a part of the company.

**Care:** Vendors should feel that the brands/retailers are invested in their growth. This motivates them. The buyer should maintain a vendor performance scorecard and work out incentives for better performance. This need not be cost-increase but may be volume-increase or technical support. The buyer should also keep the vendor in the loop for their future plans. They should also discuss improvement initiatives and give support wherever possible.

Care can also be expressed by ensuring that vendors have a single-window dealings with the company for day-to-day issues ensuring ease of business. Companies can define 'care initiatives' for the vendors, thus institutionalising this process.

There are many intangible benefits these relationships can bring like information on innovation, pricing, new launches as well as trends from other markets and companies, which can be game changing. This along with **seamlessness** & **flexibility** can completely turnaround the supply chain dynamics of a company.

One of the biggest myths in the apparel industry is assuming that the vendor is only looking for higher prices and margins.

These 4 simple principles ensure that companies attract the best vendors/ factories and create a long-term relationship which, in return, makes the vendors go that extra mile for them.

CHAPTER 4.4

# Trust-Based Supply Chains are the Future of Retail

At a time when everyone is discussing the future of sourcing in the post-COVID-19 reality, the buzzword is '**Agile**'. But agility on its own is meaningless, and it is trust that is crucial to achieve agility. In fact, in the process of putting agility as the most important requirement of the future, we are overlooking the relevance of some simple, age-old principles in an uncertain new reality – the importance of trust in supply chains, the lessons to be learnt from the unorganised sector, and how to build trust-based supply chains in the organised sector. Through this write-up, with my years of experience, I am sharing how trust can be built at the strategic and operational levels and why is it important.

The apparel industry has come a long way from the days of animal skins to smart shirts. Today, it is a force that drives significant economic development with a large impact on global GDP and is one of the main drivers of consumer behaviour worldwide. However, the supply chain is largely unorganised with few large, dominant players. In the 90's, the opening up of the economy gave rise to a prominent organised segment in apparel retail. The growth of this segment was further fueled by a shift in consumer tastes and entry of several foreign brands. Today, both segments co-exist, each contributing significantly to the market share, however with very different working styles and commitments.

## TRUST DRIVES SUPPLY CHAINS IN THE UNORGANISED SEGMENT

Over the years in the industry, I have noticed that the unorganised sector works faster and more efficiently than the organised sector. Having observed both the segments closely, I have realised that the key reason driving this is

**Trust** which is built over several years of working together, the partnership shaped by the business owners who transact directly with each other. Hence, their view of business risk is very different. For the larger players, they have the regulatory and other constraints which drive their perception of risk. Due to scale and corporatisation, the organised sector does not enjoy the benefit of such trust.

Going beyond agility to build trust in supply chains?

Being agile is about quickly responding to short-term changes in demand or supply and handling external disruptions, smoothly. This is then added with 'Strategic Adaptability' (adjusting, modifying supply networks to meet structural shifts in markets) and 'Alignment' (incentivising to business objectives) principles to drive today's supply chains. This appears to be the on-going mantra for supply chains, today.

But the question I ask is more fundamental.

**Can there be agility without trust?**

Trust between vendors and businesses lead to a bond akin to partnership, each going an extra mile for the other. This leads to a seamless supply chain, going well past the definition of agile and encompassing the principles of adaptability and alignment. I believe that trust can be built into supply chains in the organised segment as well. All retailers/brands need to relook at their functioning and inculcate certain values into their processes and systems. In my view, trust is built at two levels:

## Transactional and Strategic.

Transactional trust must be backed up by technology support. Given the large volumes of transactions, it becomes very difficult to rely on undocumented commitments. It is a risk for both parties to operate without a clear system of record. Friction is bound to happen without a technology platform, where a rogue action or a mistake by a lower-level employee can permanently damage the relationship.

Trust at the strategic level will come about only through a strong alignment of values and interests. That is much harder than merely implementing some technology. It has to be built over a long period of time, with parties standing with each other through thick & thin, almost like a marriage.

Having defined that, trust must be built first at organisational levels through clearly articulated policies and demonstrated behaviour of the senior management. These must then reflect at the operational levels with processes and behavioural principles. However, this is easier said than done and requires some basic commitments at the organisational levels.

**Building a culture based on ethics:** Businesses must instill a culture in their teams that allows an honest assessment of issues and avoids blame game on either side. Being ethical, honest and thorough will go a long way doing wonders for the relationships between vendors and customers. To put it simply, a combination of the businesses' manufacturing terms and management decisions influence how their representatives and employees identify and adjudicate issues. Moral reputation makes it easier to build trust which is then difficult to break. Being honest and thorough also helps solve problems quicker with vendors.

**Transparency in payment related issues:** It's important to realise that timely payments are crucial. It is the key to retaining and adding good suppliers. Making sure that they are paid on time will prove that the brands/retailers are reliable customers and easy to work with. If, for any reason, customers cannot make the payment on an agreed date, then informing the supplier of a revised date at the earliest is also very important.

**Consistency in words and actions:** Businesses need to have a well-articulated policy on vendor management. There should be clearly demonstrated decision-making at the top to ensure that consistency is maintained at operational levels. Vendors appreciate consistency of actions, decisions and behaviour in their relationships with the customer. While there may be short-term blips, if the long-term trend is consistent, then the relationship will thrive. No vendor likes an over opportunistic customer.

And most important – **Collaboration is the only way:** Businesses function well when all stakeholders work together, helping each other with their issues. Retailers and vendors should, cohesively, come together and build a long-term relationship. There must be a clear mechanism to set joint goals and measure achievements through a rigorous review process. This means institutionalising reviews, recognitions and celebrations. It is also important to ensure that vendors feel included in the success and growth of the company. This goes a long way in contributing to an inclusive culture.

However, these four critical commitments are not enough and what distinguishes 'trusting' from 'distrusting' relationships is the ability of the parties to make a leap of faith; they must believe that each of them is interested in the other's welfare and that neither will act without first considering their action's impact on the other.

So, while retailers may have a good intention, if it is not communicated by actions, the commitment becomes mere words. So, it is very important to build a reputation of dependability, the belief that their partners are reliable and would honour their word.

But we cannot ignore that the retailer-vendor relationships are typically imbalanced. Major retailers buy from numerous, relatively small manufacturers, and many times, the retailers position themselves as 'power centres'.

In a relationship of unequals, how can the powerful party build a trusting relationship?

The only way to create a balance is by being fair in handling this relationship. This concept includes two kinds of justice: **Distributive** and **Procedural**.

Distributive justice deals with the fair distribution of the pie. In all practicality, it implies that the rewards and the responsibilities are distributed judicially to all the stakeholders. This needs to be managed through a process of joint reviews of commitment to each other's success.

On the other hand, procedural justice relates to the fairness of the partnership management mechanism of the dominant faction. This should allow for a mechanism to manage refutability, implying that retailers should build a culture in which a vendor can reach out comfortably to anyone in the organisation, be it other departments or senior management, without backlash from the operational teams. This is also the vendors' mental cushion.

Another very important aspect of behavioural trust comes from '**Familiarity**' and '**Courtesy**'. Strong relationships are established when people interact. In this respect, an effort by the retailers to learn more about their vendors is often fruitful. The various functions such as buyers, merchandisers, designers, etc. must visit the organisation of the vendors.

This helps break the ice between the teams and create mutual respect. Relationships, thus, formed are long-lasting and encourage trust.

Courtesy is cornerstone of a good retailer/supplier partnership. Treating a vendor partner with respect and modesty is crucial to building the interpersonal relationship. Ultimately, relationships between companies are relationships between teams of people on either side. We should not forget that in an ever-changing business environment, a seamless supply chain, built on trust, is the need of the hour.

# PART 5

# MY SOURCING JOURNAL

***Sourcing is not an easy task, and this journal teaches you what not many people will!***

Over time, my journal has been filled with many tidbits about what ought to be done and what not… These chapters in the fifth part are nothing but extracts from my past, which are key learnings and lessons I want to pass on to all.

CHAPTER 5.1

# Does Anyone Plan in Sourcing?

In most cases, the onus of delivery delays lies with the sourcing team, for they are the link between the brand and the vendors/manufacturers, accountable to get goods into the warehouse on time. And when asked why the delays occurred, the sourcing team invariably gets into emotional discussions and go through hundreds of emails, trying to figure out when & what went wrong. In this exclusive article, written for Apparel Resources by Anindya Ray, Chief Sourcing Officer, Arvind highlights some major aspects that help companies in better planning.

## Have you ever witnessed what delayed deliveries do to business?

In the apparel industry, most of us have witnessed it. But, unfortunately, no one calculates the actual loss to business due to this. Instead, it leads to emotional changes and counter charges. It is this lack of accountability for lost opportunities, which essentially does not allow for measurement, hence there are no improvements that can be seen.

You may think that I am being harsh; but am I really? Why, otherwise, is the sourcing landscape so cluttered and chaotic?

**Delay in delivery** is commonly heard in our daily lives. All business functions are affected by these, from the merchandisers to the sales staff.

That happens because instead of planning and monitoring a Time and Action Calendar (TNA), the sourcing team works on vendor promises, commitments and prayers to God.

**If we were to analyse the sourcing function, it's nothing but simple project management and TNA is that planning tool which helps and enables**

**efficiencies.** It highlights issues on a timely basis and allows for proactive measures to be taken, minimising losses for the organisations.

The benefits of the TNA are immense, yet for some reason, it's not utilised to its potential in our industry.

To understand the TNA better, we need to understand the **3 components of sourcing** which keep this machine rolling.

3 Components of Sourcing

*original infographic created by Aninyda Ray

**PREPARE**: Ensure all pre-production planning is in place for example, gold seals, tech packs, approvals, counter quotes, compliance checks and vendor partner selection. Make sure that the orders are all actionable and not some excel sheet that's mailed across; there should be no gaps in data.

**PLAN**: Ensure that fabric/yarns are all pre-planned, capacities with mills are blocked, vendor capacities are taken well in advance and commercials are closed. And most importantly, backward planning for all timelines is done from the targeted delivery date and this plan (TNA) is confirmed with the vendor.

**PROGRESS**: Monitor the plan daily, create checkpoints and take proactive measures to ensure delivery is on time.

TNA is a tool that takes care of all pillars of sourcing and helps a merchandiser keep track of orders through the manufacturing process.

From preparing to planning to monitoring progress, a TNA helps in organising the workflow, ensuring that issues are dealt with proactively and do not cause business losses. It's the best tool a merchandiser can equip himself with to ensure the smooth flow of all orders.

## Why do we need a TNA?

The apparel industry is a complex one and sourcing apparel products is even more so.

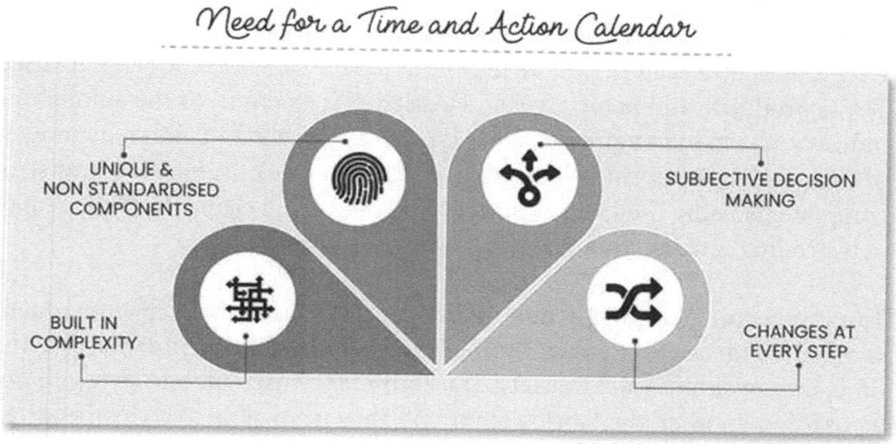


*original infographic created by Aninyda Ray

## Built-In Complexity

In a year, we deal with 2-4 seasons, which are further divided into monthly drops. And the total number of styles per month may vary based on the size of the brand, categories the brand caters to and the sub-brands it has. In essence, a merchandiser has to deal with about 100-200 styles, each at different stages of the manufacturing process, with a different end date. Each of these styles have 20-30 different components such as fabrics, interlining, buttons, thread, labels, and many more…

So, a merchandiser is dealing with about 2000/6000 components, each of which is important and can impact the delivery. For example, if the correct thread is not supplied on time, the garment cannot be stitched. If the washing chemical is not supplied on time, the garment cannot be finished. Even something like a hangtag can lead to delays.

Adding further to this complexity is the fact that every product is unique and most of the components cannot be standardised.

## Unique And Non-Standardised Components

The fact that fashion companies, by default, and designs keep changing a majority of the products in every drop, leading to so much variety that they end up using many unique and non-standardised components in the products. Each style we make has something unique of its own which makes standardisation of all components rather difficult.

If we look at other industries, we may find that the same components are used across products, and many are standardised. For example, in the automobile industry, the same engine, chassis, tyres may be used in different models of cars. Only the outside elements may change, minimising the number of components being used, hence simplifying the supply chain. Also, the rate of new product introduction is nowhere close to fashion.

This is unfortunately not possible in the apparel industry for every component is visible and impacts the consumer's decision-making. And most of the time, the consumer wants variety. The embroidery used on one style will not be used on another, the fabric colour will vary from style to style, the stripe pattern will be different, and so on.

The merchandiser is actually dealing with multiple unique components on a daily basis, and what makes this further difficult is the fact that the decisions making isn't easy.

## Subjective Decision-Making

'This is not the right shade of blue', 'this button does not look good', 'this embroidery is not aesthetically pleasing'...We have all said or heard these words often. For most of the decisions, made in the apparel industry, are marred by subjectivity. There is no right or wrong, it's just a matter of perspective, derived from individual experiences. Now, imagine the impact this causes on the supply chain!

Most of the times, merchandisers don't even know if the fabric is the right shade, or the embroidery looks aesthetically pleasing. This subjectivity also leads to multiple changes.

## Changes At Every Step

Subjective decision-making, changing consumer preferences, market insights, or last-minute add-on requirements – all of these have an impact on the apparel supply chain. And it's imperative that these are addressed.

These add to the built-in complexity of this supply chain, making it difficult for the merchandiser to always keep track. These decisions are, in most cases, taken by people who are not even a part of the process such as designers, sales teams, business heads, etc.

This subjectivity is one of the unique problems of this supply chain.

Given this complexity, it's humanly impossible to remember everything by the merchandisers. No amount of to-dos, emails and lists can help organise. Yet, I have always noticed that the merchandisers tend to plot everything in their minds and expect things to flow smoothly. And experience tells us that anything that can go wrong, will go wrong. Hence, I always maintain – **the only way this business can function is by planning a TNA and following it like law…**

Once the order flows in, the TNA should be plotted and calendarised. Then, it's a matter of tracking it daily, and proactively solving any problems before they arise. It's only with a TNA plan that a merchandiser can anticipate these problems and ensure they do not hinder the delivery of the product, ensuring a smooth business flow.

It's all so common-sense and of course everyone does it. So, why are we even discussing it? The reality is that if you really ask sourcing merchants for their TNA, most will look blank and the few that do have it may not be updating it regularly.

What is the problem that people have with 'planning'? I don't know, but it is simply not done. Maybe, they feel it will throw up new challenges by exposing the risk factors, hence, increasing mental anxiety and work. Or maybe people simply like to be paper-pushers, doing a postman's job…That way if anything goes wrong, it's always someone else's problem.

The main thing is '**ownership**'. If sourcing teams have ownership, they will 'plan' for success. And I have seen that if the planning is done properly, it's 80 per cent success with in-time deliveries and quality. But it's when they allow vendors to dictate their fate that companies suffer.

Unfortunately, Indian companies and their CEOs do not spend adequate time on sourcing and supply chain. This in turn leads to the apathy we see in the back end today.

CHAPTER 5.2

# Selecting the Right Vendor

Over my many years in this industry, my journal has amassed quite a few pages which are about my day-to-day learnings at work.

These learnings today have become **unique insights into this industry and its functioning**.

When people asked me to write something about sourcing, I decided to peek into my journal and share a few of my insights.

A **vendor is one of the main stakeholders of our business**, hence my first chapter in this series is about:

## Selecting the Right Vendor

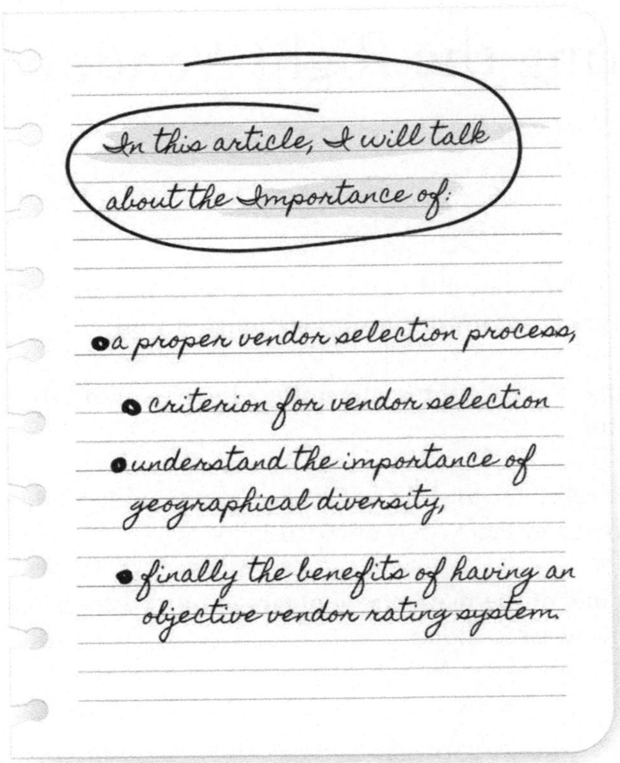


How important is it to select the right vendor? How often do we go with the vendors we are comfortable with? The ones we know will offer us least resistance in terms of last-minute changes and slip ups, and will cover for us during reviews.

So, this brings us to the question,

### How important is it to select the right vendor and how does one do it?

It's important to stress the criticality to study the geographical spread of factories. For easy example, split the country into four zones - north, east, south, west. Identify key category hubs in each region and decide the percentage split in desired business from these hubs.

This decision can be based on cost, product handwriting, logistical ease, capacity, regional stability to name some.

It's important to also de-risk the business by ensuring that each category is well-balanced in capacity allocation. So, if there are any major disturbances in a region, it does not impact the whole business and one can localise the impact.

Once done, look at developing factories or placing business in these hubs. The same applies internationally as well - specialisation, cost, duties and lead times play a major role in the decision. It's always good to revisit this regularly and set clear targets for de-risking and optimising before getting into vendor selection.

## What should we look for in vendor selection?

It's always good to develop a points-based vendor rating system which allows for objective assessment and unbiased decision-making. These points should be from different stakeholders in the system, like finance, quality, compliance, sourcing and product/design teams.

It's good to even look at taking feedback from raw material vendors to understand the culture of the vendor.

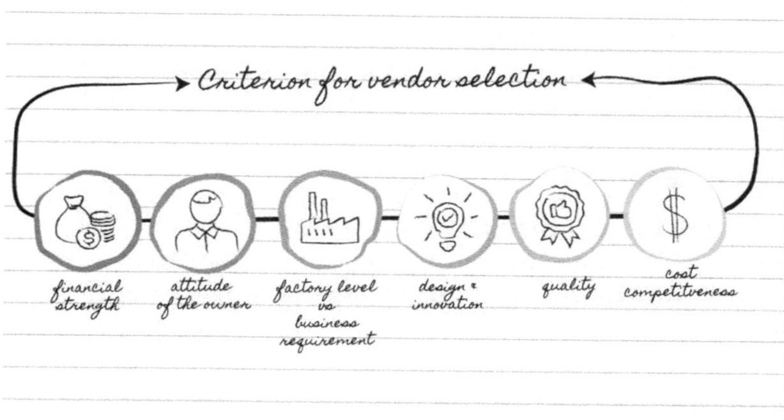

## Having said this, let's look at some of the criterion for vendor selection:

### Financial Strength

The first question to ask is - if the vendor has the financial capability to manage his working capital. The most critical point being - can he manage an additional month of working capital stress? It's important that a month-wise investment plan is worked every season with the vendor before deciding volumes to be placed with him.

### Attitude of the Owner

How is the vendor's attitude towards business ethics? Is he too stuck up with his idea of working or is he open to new ways of doing business? Is he the kind of vendor one can build a long term commitment with? All businesses have ups and downs - can we count on the vendor's support during such times.

### Factory Level versus the Business Requirement

Is there possibility of growth? What kind of internal quality processes does the factory have? Is there some basic compliance in place? Is the factory capable of investing in ethical, sustainable business practices? Does the business have the capability of going online and digitally managing the business?

### Design and Innovation

What kind of design and innovation support is the factory capable of giving? Is the factory investing in innovation and sampling? This becomes very important as we keep moving to value added products.

### Cost Competitiveness

What is the cost structure of the factory? How has the factory invested in efficiency and cost management? How good is the factory's own sourcing capability for raw materials? These continue to be one of the key driving factors.

### Quality

Can the factory become a green channel quality resource in the next one year? Such factories should be prioritised over others. Ideally 30-40% factories should be green channel in the complete supply chain.

Having discussed the above, it would be important to understand the following aspects as well like: Management control of vendor base (defining an optimal span of control by number of vendors being managed) is as important as keeping an ongoing vendor development plan to ensure that there are always new vendors being identified, assessed and kept future ready.

And finally, I cannot emphasise enough on the importance of a **seasonal audit** and making it the key deciding factor in placing business. This will ensure a seasonal vendors' review that will allow vendors at the bottom of the rating system to be either replaced or given a warning and pushed to improve.

A lot of people will say, what about other teams wanting their vendors or urgent requirements, when there are no capacities blocked. Well, if you are diligently following this way of working, it's never going to be an issue. Just remember - as long as you clearly define a span of control, introducing a new vendor will mean taking another one out.

These were some simple pointers to creating a relevant and robust vendor base. What do you think?

CHAPTER 5.3

# A Clean Sourcing Organisation - Is it Really Possible?

I started writing chapters to share my learnings and experiences. To that end, I like discussing subjects that most people don't talk about. This topic came about because a person, who is new to the industry, but quite senior, recently told me that he had heard that this industry had an integrity issue.

That set me thinking. And I don't want to get defensive, but the fact is that it is very important to ensure, through processes and practices, that there is none or very little opportunity for leaks in the system.

In this chapter, I will share some good practices that I have seen over the years. Loosely put, this chapter is divided into,

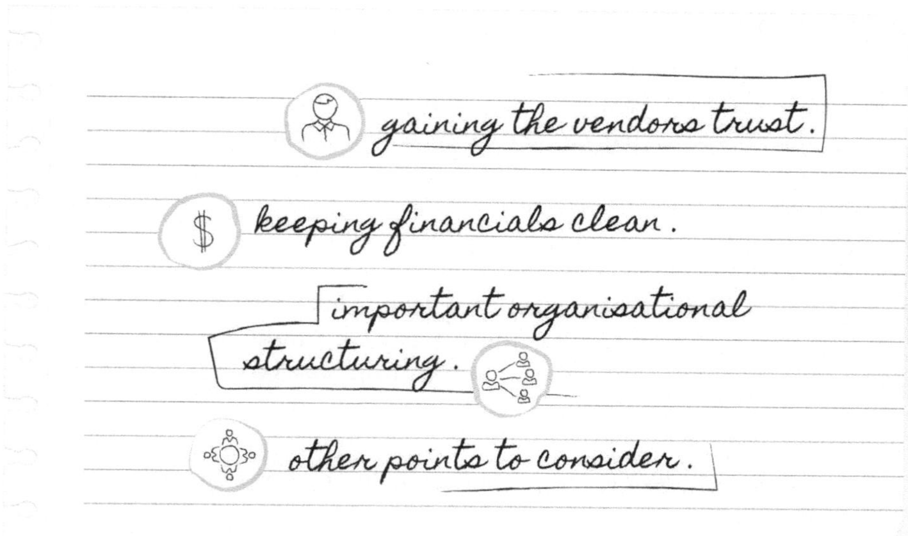

I understand that these processes and steps cannot be implemented at scale, in one go. This holds true for large companies as well as mid-size ones. To that end, I would recommend that financials be given the most importance, followed by vendor trust and lastly, organisational structure.

However, let's start by understanding **Why and How to Gain the Vendors' Trust**.

## Gaining The Vendors' Trust

The vendors are the most important piece in this effort, and it is important to ensure that they feel secure against backlash and be guaranteed of fair play. Mostly, vendors deal with junior and mid-level executives in the company and are at their mercy for business. Hence, the following is very important in creating trust.

### Build Senior Management Connect with Vendors

Senior Management should regularly interact with vendors and sometimes, directly ask them about their interaction with the company. Mostly, at that time, vendors may not respond but may well come back, anonymously or will know that they can approach the senior management team.

### Build A Redressal Mechanism

This will allow vendors to anonymously approach or complain without fear of backlash. It could be done using a drop box or some online complaint recording platform. But the important thing here is to ensure that the complainant is protected, and the complainant's identity is not revealed. Very few people come forward to complain and their interest must be protected.

### External Intelligence Gathering

Large companies can have their own teams, but smaller to medium sized organisations should utilise third party organisations that could do surveillance, study financial etc., in case of reportage or suspicion. Do not leave it to internal reviews and discussion.

Having done this, it's then important to build processes that help in,

## Keeping The Financials Clean

It is important to understand the potential leak points and then putting in robust processes to manage those. These processes should be independently managed by a resource, ideally attached to the finance team, who manages this data and independently ensures that these processes are enforced.

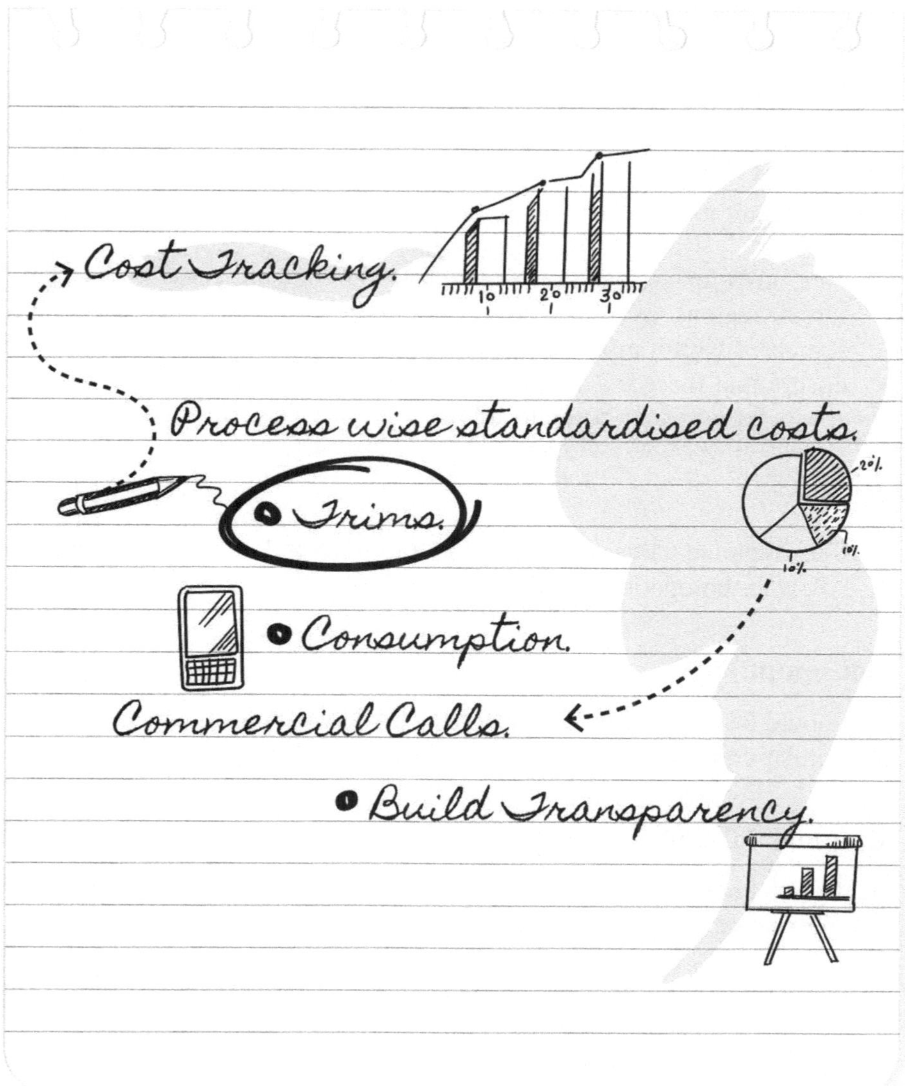

## Cost Tracking

This should be managed in the following manner:

- Putting in place a **core business - price tracking mechanism** with a minimum of 3 years data availability. This should be backed by a dual region, cost comparison and ideal placement.
- Ensure **zero-based costing - for fashion**. With reasonable sample sizes being taken through multiple costings (cross costings) for the same style.

## Process-wise Standardised Costs

It is important to negotiate and maintain,

- Rate cards for various processes across vendors and comparative charts across regions as well. These should be separately negotiated and compared within minimum two regions.
- Ensure that there is a scientifically done SMV's and process mapping to ensure back ups for cost allocations.

## Trims

- Keep regional trims vendors and a minimum of 2 or 3 for each region.
- Allow for competitive bidding in trims.

## Consumption

- Should be CAD based. Separately verified by tech team.
- Similar consumptions compared between vendors.

## Commercial Calls

As we all know that there are many commercial calls taken during the manufacturing process, these should be managed on 3 levels:

- The Company or Business head or
- Sourcing/Category head or
- Quality/Category head

These calls should ideally not be taken by the junior merchants on their own.

## Build Transparency

- Ensure all cost breakdowns are in a common system with access to other stakeholders in the company as well.

It is good to reiterate once more that financial processes need to be kept robust and independently monitored. Now it is important to understand how to support this through proper organisational structuring.

## Important Organisational Structuring

These are simple, yet very effective in ensuring that processes and relationships are kept professional.

## Job Rotation

It is very important that there is job rotation at junior levels.

- Yearly rotation of quality auditors (QA).
- And, at least, a two-yearly rotation of Sourcing Merchant.

This avoids familiarity and keeps the relationships professional.

## Gifting Policy

Most companies have vague policies or maybe policies like 'no gifts'. But these should be calibrated well, as every country has unique cultures and policies, and one should recognise and be sensitive towards the same. For example, flowers, cards or sweets may be acceptable in some cultures and refusing those may be insulting to others. But clear guidelines must be put in place to avoid ambiguity.

## Some Other Points To Consider Are:

## Regular Financial Audit

This is a must and should be fully enabled and supported. I have noticed that most financial auditors stick to basic procurement logic, but it is important for them to understand the nuances of the industry as mentioned in the financials' section. These should be audited keeping those aspects in mind as well.

To conclude, I will say that - what really matters is the culture created in the team. It should be one of meritocracy and transparency, process and data-driven. This must be led from the top by the senior management team, through demonstrative leadership.

CHAPTER 5.4

# The Much-maligned T&A in Sourcing

Having spent many years in the Apparel industry, I have come across multiple situations where organisations have lost business due to delay in deliveries. The onus of this delay lies on the sourcing team, and, invariably, they do not seem to have objective answers. All we get are emotional responses.

When asked about Time and Action Calendar (T&A), mails and words are shown to the stakeholders instead of an actionable plan.

I have always wondered why this happens!

The basis of any sourcing organisation/team to function well, is planning and a T&A is the heart of that planning process which keeps everything on track.

Hence, I have taken up this topic in the series – '**My Sourcing Journal**'.

In this article I will discuss in detail:

- Pillars of the sourcing function
- Why apparel sourcing needs a T&A
- Why merchandisers shy away from it
- Basis of a good T&A
- Tips to manage the T&A, and
- Digitisation of T&A and making it a management tool

Let's begin by first understanding the pillars of the sourcing function, namely:

1. **Preparation** refers to pre-production planning that includes counter quotes, prior approvals and selecting the right partners who would, therein, ensure timely delivery along with quality.
2. **Planning** is ensuring that every variable is taken care of. Right vendor is allocated with the right product and all variables like costs closures, approvals, fabrics orders, trims etc., are in place.
3. Once the preparation and planning are in place, monitoring the **Progress** is the key to ensuring success.

T&A plays a role in all the above as creating the plan and execution monitoring is the essence of sourcing, yet it is the most ignored.

A simple tool like T&A does wonders in organising the workflow and ensuring that issues are dealt proactively, without impacting the business adversely.

While we speak about the importance of T&A, it's pertinent that we understand its importance specifically in the apparel industry.

## So, Why Does Apparel Sourcing Need a T&A?

Apparel industry is a complex one, and sourcing products even more so.

Many a times, we see changes happening during the manufacturing process like changing embroidery, wash and similar parameters. Some of these decisions may be last minute calls, taken by people who may not even be a part of the process, such as designers, sales teams and business heads. This subjectivity is one of the unique problems of this supply chain.

At any given point, a merchandiser deals with 100-200 styles, each style consisting of 20/30 variables. In essence, we are talking about each merchandiser managing about 5000/6000 variables - variables like fabrics, trim fabrics, buttons, interlinings and many more.

I have never understood why merchandisers tend to rely on their minds to manage this complexity. Invariably, they plot everything in their minds and expect things to flow smoothly. And as we know from experience, in sourcing, anything that can go south, will.

**REALISTICALLY SPEAKING, THE ONLY WAY OUR BUSINESS CAN FUNCTION SMOOTHLY IS CHARTING OUT A T&A AND FOLLOWING IT.**

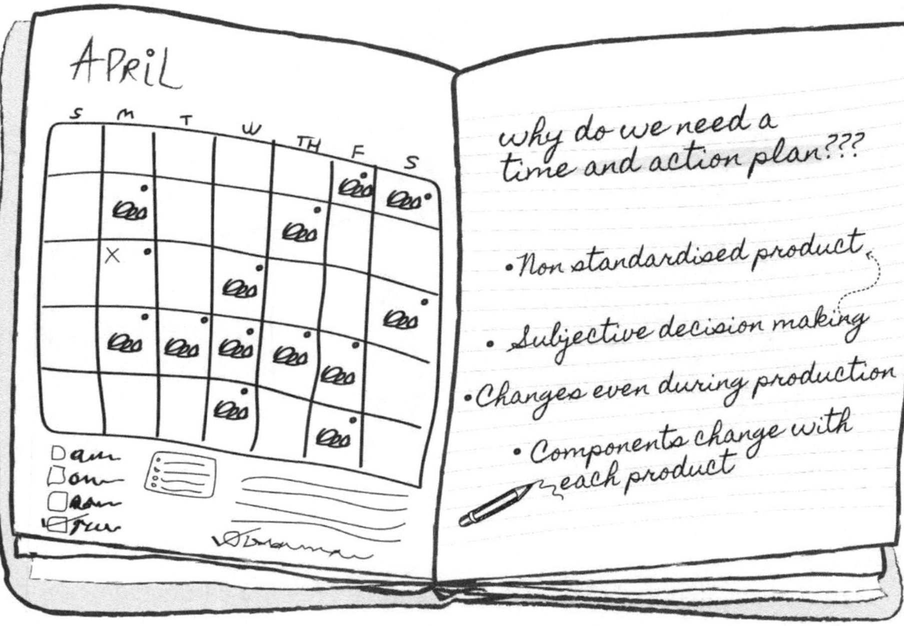


Apparel products are ever-changing and so are its variables. If we look at other industries, many of these variables are standardised.

For example, in automobile manufacturing, the same engine, chassis, tyre may be used to produce many different models of cars. Here, only the superficial elements change, minimising the number of variables used.

In apparel manufacturing, however, everything changes, every time. For example, fabric, sewing thread, buttons to interlinings change from one style to another, hence a T&A is of the utmost importance in our industry.

While we understand that the T&A is the backbone of sourcing, we see many merchandisers resist using this tool.

Many believe that updating and maintaining T&A is a cumbersome process and often takes up a lot of their working hours.

The T&A begins with planning in minute details many different variables and then updating the progress against these variables on a periodical basis. This requires a lot of discipline, and it becomes a reason behind the merchandisers' resistance towards it.

If used properly, working hours will reduce by 50%. If the T&A is shared with everyone, it cuts down unnecessary meetings, reviews and updates. The data is available with everyone, and things move smoothly.

## Basis of a Good T&A

Ours is a very old industry and many buying houses, exporters, sourcing businesses have reached great success by keeping the T&A as the backbone of their businesses.

One of the best practices to overcome the inertia and resistance towards the T&A is to create a simple work discipline within the merchandising team.

- **1st hour** - spent going through the emails and actioning out the urgent and important ones.
- **2nd hour** - spent updating the T&A which in turn tells the merchandiser the priorities and the action points for the day.
- **Last hour** of the day - spent responding to all the emails and queries which have come in during the day.

As the T&A is updated every day, the critical aspects start falling into place and work gets aligned. This is typically how a merchandiser's day should look like.

## Some Tips to Manage the T&A:

- Most people keep changing the end date when there is a delay and then map the actuals. One must understand that the end date is sacrosanct. The right way to go about this is to ensure a missed deadline doesn't impact the end date. If one deadline is missed, the key thing is to catch the next deadline.

The real job of the merchandiser is to create the T&A, monitor it closely and come up with solutions when a deadline is missed, ensuring the end date is not changed.

- A tip I always share is to chase the PCD or the 'planned cut date'. If a factory cuts the product at the right date, there are minimal chances of delay in the delivery. A factory will only cut the product when all its variables are in place. Once it has cut the product, it is not going to hold it and wait. This will automatically ensure that the product moves out of the factory as soon as possible.

- Regular reviews, maintaining T&A hygiene and accuracy, and updating it every week are some of the key areas which a sourcing organisation needs to focus on.

## Digitisation Of T&A And Making It A Management Tool

Today, with digitisation becoming a mainstay, there are systems built around T&A. Many PLM tools systemise the T&A to an extent where it automatically creates actionable points for management. Within the system, an escalation matrix is created, which eases out the work process for everyone. It allows for transparency between all stakeholders making everyone proactive and keeping delays in check.

To conclude, sourcing is like project management and T&A is the perfect tool to enable efficiencies.

Once an order is placed, we decide on an end date/delivery date and work backwards to decide on milestones to meet this end date. These milestones must be aligned with the various stakeholders to execute the product in the stipulated time.

Once this is calendarised, it's just a matter of ensuring each milestone is met. And in case of delays, proactive measures need to be taken.

I believe that T&A management and adopting digital systems to do is the key to succeeding in a sourcing team/organisation.

CHAPTER 5.5

# Regional or Centralised - What Really Works!

**Sourcing is, undeniably, the backbone of our industry. This function is the one that gives shape to the designer's vision and creates that tangible product the consumers buy.**

In India, we have many manufacturing hubs, like Ludhiana, Delhi, Kolkata, Salem, Tirupur and many more, yet we usually have one sourcing team sitting in the HO trying to source from one place.

But the fundamental question I ask is - **Should sourcing be centralised?**

While I am very sure that there are merits to a centralised sourcing function, I believe, it's a regional sourcing model that creates real value in this business. Hence, I have taken up this topic as the fIfth article in this series – '**My Sourcing Journal**'.

In this article I will discuss in detail:

- Types of sourcing structures
- Regional sourcing teams & its advantages
- Developing regional sourcing teams as business centres

Our industry has many different players - big, small and medium sized brands/retailers who have different sourcing models.

Let's first understand what these different sourcing models are.

The below infographic clearly indicates the different models that exist.

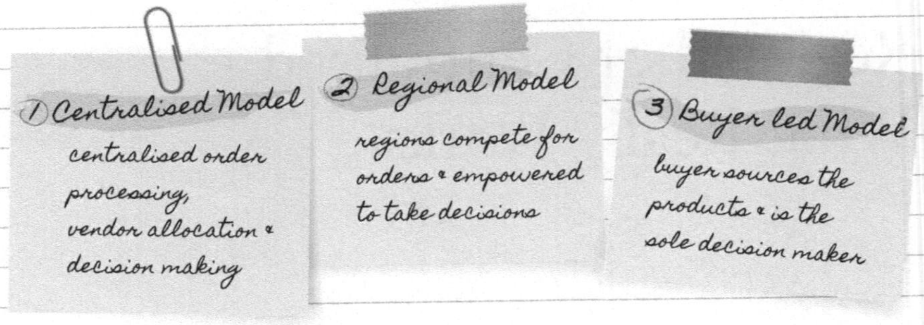


Each of these models have their own merits and demerits. While a centralised sourcing model helps in consolidation of vendor base, a regional model offers varied products at effective costs.

There is no right or wrong sourcing model, and each business needs to take a call based on its own requirements.

For many big brands/retailers, who have requirements of varied products across different categories, it's very important to source from different regions and build a strong regional sourcing model.

So, what are the **advantages of regional sourcing model**?

- Each region or manufacturing hub has an expertise unique to them. For example, knits from Kolkata have a higher lustre due to the softness of water in the region which impacts the dying process. Delhi specialises in hand embroideries, Salem in cotton fabrics and so on. This expertise is so unique to the region that, in most cases, it cannot be replicated elsewhere. Hence, it is very important to diversify and create a regional sourcing model, particularly for the big brands/retailers.
- Having a diverse geographic mix in vendor base de-risks business. If sourcing is focused or concentrated in a few hubs, then it is susceptible to calamities or geopolitical upheavals that can have a negative impact on the supply chain. We can take the example of the recent pandemic, where brands with concentrated sourcing hubs, have seen a negative impact on their supply chain.

To keep businesses on track, even when there may be a natural calamity, it is important to distribute the sourcing of products across regions. This creates a safety net and helps brands/retailers wade through difficult times without any hiccups.

A regional sourcing model builds competitive advantage within the organisation and benefits the brands/retailers by:

1. Creating competition for orders amongst the different regional teams
2. Building access to specialised vendors across region
3. Giving effective cost benefits

We usually see that brands/retailers go with a centralised sourcing model. They believe that a centralised team builds economies of scale. It helps in creating better control over the supply chain & logistics and consolidating vendor base.

Consolidation of vendor base is good but should be done sensibly keeping regionality and product specialisation in mind.

While most big brands/retailers source from multiple regions, they limit decision-making to the central team.

The regional teams are mere assistants, following up on orders, having no decision-making powers. In most cases, this builds many wasteful days into the actual lead times as samples and all are sent to and fro for approvals.

## REGIONAL SOURCING TEAMS SHOULD ACTUALLY BE BUSINESS CENTRES AND NOT MERE ASSISTANTS.

When regional sourcing teams become business centres, they will compete and

- Find new factories
- Negotiate better costs and payment terms
- Study the competition
- Ensure timely deliveries
- Build a competent vendor base

But for regional sourcing teams to become business centres, they need to be empowered to make decisions, approve samples, finalise vendors, decide which orders to take etc.

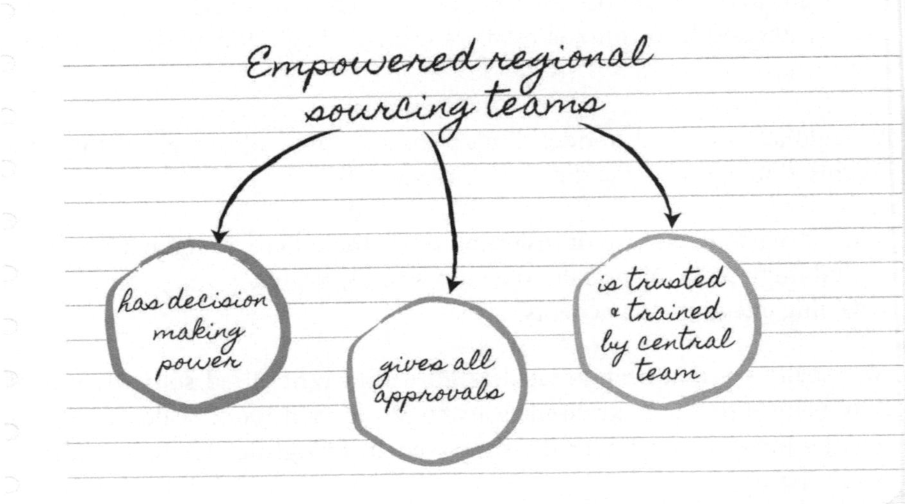


An empowered regional sourcing team saves time with on-the-spot approvals and quick decision-making, making the supply chain agile.

To empower them, it is important that the regional sourcing teams are trained well by the central team. This builds trust between the teams and helps in smoother transition of orders. It should also be ensured that the regional team's KRA is a combination of OTIF and business turnover.

An empowered regional sourcing team doesn't just deliver quick results and create business impact, it also removes a lot of burden from the central sourcing team. In fact, in many cases, a small central sourcing team and a QA team is all that's required, while the regional team takes charge.

Of course, the regional sourcing model has some demerits as highlighted below.

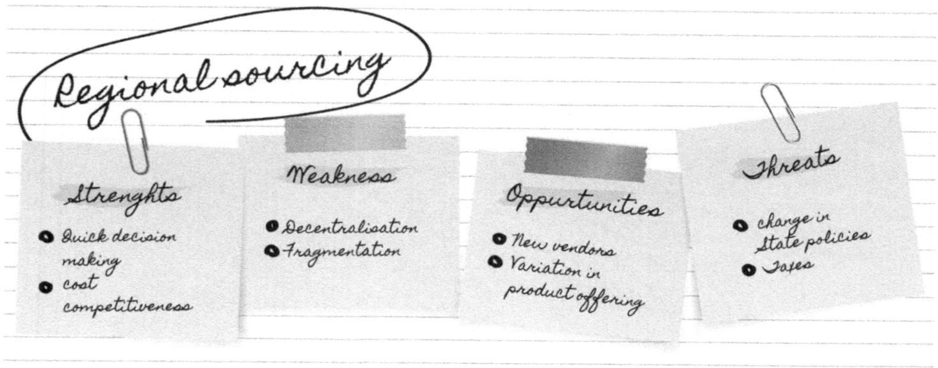


But the merits, by far, outweigh the demerits and create a value win situation for the brands/retailers.

I believe that regional sourcing model is the way for the future and it's important that brands/retailers start making this shift to build strong, empowered regional teams.

CHAPTER 5.6

# Reducing Cogs - The Eternal Quest!

COGS! - The '**Direct costs of producing the good sold**' by any company.

It is a term we are all familiar with. And the quest to 'Reduce Cogs' is one of the key deliverables of any sourcing organisation. All companies look first at the sourcing function when it comes to reducing the COGS.

But the question I ask here is - **Is it just the responsibility of the Sourcing function?**

I believe, it is the collaborative responsibility of different functions, and they can empower the sourcing team to deliver better results. Hence, I have taken up this topic as the sixth article in this series – '**My Sourcing Journal**'.

Here I will discuss in detail:

- Factors influencing COGS
- Sourcing controlled factors of COGS
- How design and buying teams can influence COGS
- Hidden costs which need attention

COGS may be a simple four-letter term, but its impact on any business is considerably high. There are many different factors influencing costs and each needs to be looked at closely under a lens. It is an interplay of many different factors. Some of which are directly controlled by the sourcing team.

Let's first understand the factors that are controlled by the sourcing function directly and how they can economise and impact the cogs.

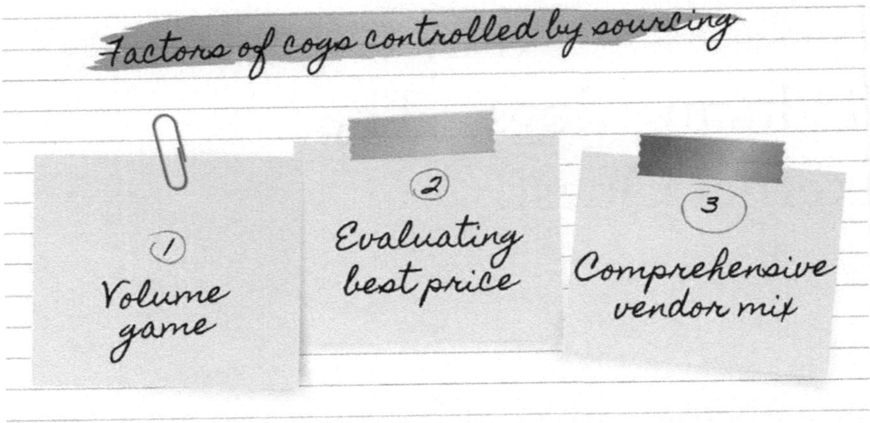


## 1. Play The Volume Game

Volume, in business, has a direct impact on costs of the products. Higher the volume, lower the costs. Hence, **volume bundling** has a big impact on the costs. This bundling can be done by consolidating orders across brands/ sub-brands and business units. It helps in achieving scale in production and improving efficiency, thereby lowering the costs.

**Consolidating the vendor base** within and across business units also helps in achieving scale, as orders are not fragmented across too many vendors.

## 2. Evaluating Best Price

This involves granular cost-visibility through **open-costing** and internal **standardisation of rate cards** across processes and functions.

Cost transparency leads to **analytics-driven best-price evaluation**, which keeps the emotion and the comfort levels out of the negotiation and price evaluation. Today, we can also rely on digital tools and advance data analytics techniques to evaluate the costs.

Another aspect to consider here is **establishing a competitive bidding process** to get the best prices. This opens the orders to multiple vendors, and each compete to get the business in. Sometimes, it makes sense to do this, within the established vendor base, allowing processes and quality to remain untouched. This gives rise to the competitive spirit in vendors. However, care must be taken to ensure that vendors do not cartelise to take prices up, hence a hybrid between existing vendors and a few new ones is probably a good practice.

**Nomination of yarns, fabrics and trims** helps in further ensuring that costs are managed across the value chain and that one benefits of scale through consolidation of raw materials across the vendor base.

### 3. Create A Comprehensive Vendor Mix

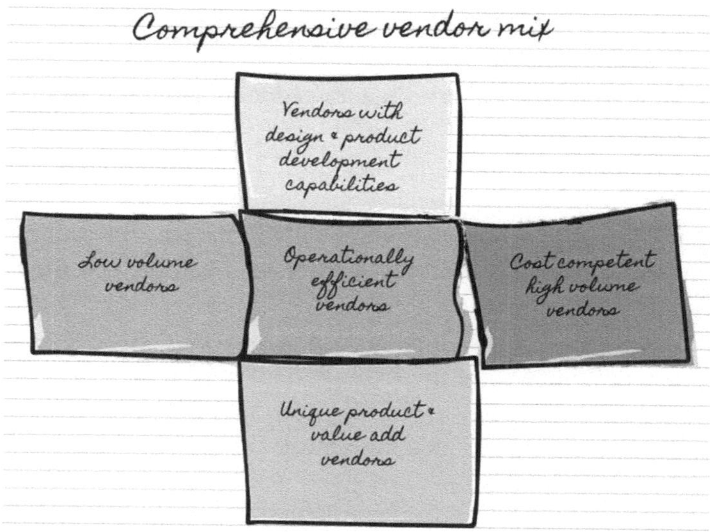


Each vendor has different strengths and weaknesses. Some may have design capabilities but higher costs while others may have exceptional operational efficiency but provide no market intel.

The vendor's strengths should be assessed, and a comprehensive vendor mix should be created based on the need of the business and what the vendor is bringing to the table, not necessarily only on cost.

The order allocation and bidding should be done based on these vendor capabilities. For eg: core products could be allocated to low-cost vendors, while a product with special features should be given to a vendor specialising in the same, irrespective of cost competitiveness.

Another aspect to be investigated is to ensure regional diversity of the vendor base. A **regionally diverse vendor base** gives an organisation a competitive advantage. While it safeguards them against many issues (refer to previous article), it also creates a unique competitive environment and helps to play on the region's strengths.

Ensuring an optimal distribution across sourcing hubs, with diverse offerings, is very important. One region may have advantages which the other region lacks, and this advantage is passed on to the brands in the form of costs.

Undeniably, the sourcing team plays a major role in determining the COGS in a business.

But is it the only function responsible for reducing and optimising it?

The answer is no!

There are other factors which play an equally important role but outside the purview of the sourcing team. This is where the Design and Buying teams step in.

The designers and buyers are the foundation of any apparel business. Many factors, when controlled at the conception stage, can economise the costs. These are directly influenced by the design and buying teams.

## Factors Influenced By The Buying And Design Teams And How They Impact Cogs

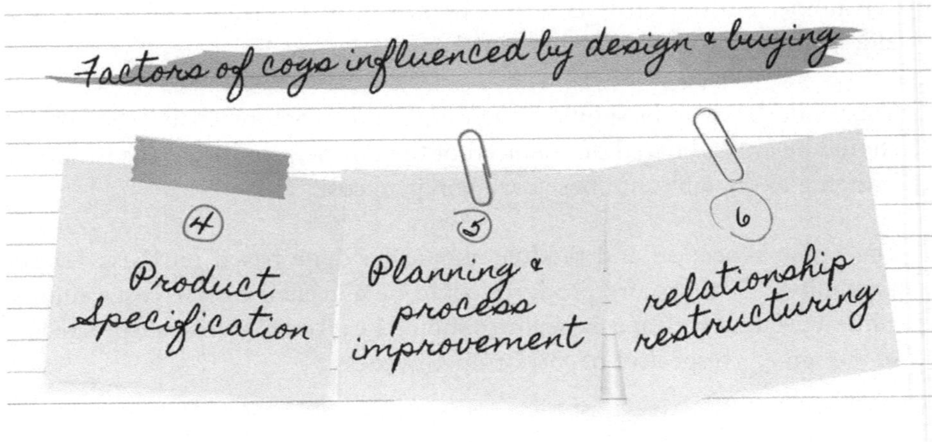

## 4. Product Specification

Product specification comes from the designer and **building a design led cost control mechanism** helps in reducing COGS effectively.

Small shifts in design process, as demonstrated in below infographic, have a big impact on the costs.

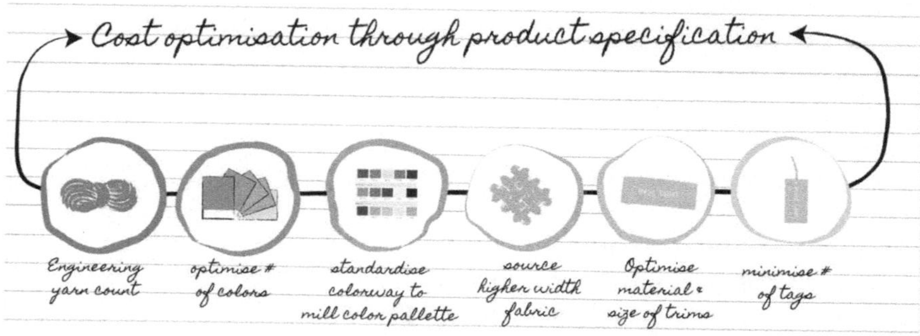


**Standardising product components** like fabrics, trims, tags etc further adds to it.

Clubbed with **optimised buying depths**, through regulation-controlled design width, based on analytics, help in building scale and achieving component as well as garment MOQ's. Thereby, reducing COGS.

## 5. Planning & Process Improvement

Due to the seasonal nature of the apparel industry, manufacturing capacity is under-utilised during **lean periods.** The buying teams can use this to their advantage and plan production of core/all year-round products at this time. The vendors usually give lower costs to keep their production capacities occupied.

Another important aspect in planning is, **fabric platforming and forward buying**. Based on historical data and trend analysis, the buyers can book griege fabrics, core fabrics, yarns etc. which offsets increase in raw material prices. A low hanging fruit is to take advantage of platforming across departments, standardising a certain minimum percentage of designs through platformed bases.

Sampling cost is an often neglected one which is built into the final COGS. Utilising technology and **shifting to digital sampling and prototyping** also reduces number of iterations, costs along with building other efficiencies into the process.

## 6. Relationship Restructuring

Along-with diversity of vendors, it is also important to **optimise the buy model itself**. How much are buying through agents, how much through direct FOB, imports, specialised vendors for value added products? This has a direct impact of cost, quality and delivery effectiveness.

All these factors, whether controlled by sourcing or influenced by the design and buying teams, are not mutually exclusive.

They are interdependent and a collaborative interplay, required to impact COGS - a responsibility to be borne by all the three functions. If platforming and cost optimisation is done at the design stage itself, then leveraging them becomes easier which benefits the overall business.

Any organization, which is looking to impact COGS, must develop a strategic sourcing plan based on the above factors.

The factors charted above are some of the big-ticket items, strategising which will have an immediate impact on the COGS. But what one overlooks are the hidden costs. These may appear to be of lesser consequence, but further examination shows that they do have a substantial cumulative impact.

## Which Are These Hidden Costs?

### Transportation

Managing inwards logistics through strategic third party tie ups may prove efficient and cost-effective as against fragmented vendor managed deliveries.

### Consumptions

Standardising fits and specs across brands and sub-brands have an impact on reducing the COGS as well as improved consumer experience. Having a technical team with CAD's to back up consumptions and resolve disputes, scientifically, helps.

### Trims

Trims account for 12-15% of the costs, and yet this is an area which is often ignored. We over engineer these at product level but they have no actual relevance to the end consumer, often landing in garbage bins.

Questioning the purpose of each trim and eliminating the unnecessary ones is a way to reduce costs. Also, harmonising trim specs across brands and sub-brands helps in bringing down the costs.

### Manpower Savings

This is an often-ignored area, as it does not impact COGS directly. But **creating GREEN CHANNEL factories** reduces manpower requirement. Also, **increasing the scope field quality team**, for factory follow ups and reporting, can ease out a lot of the manpower required for this work at the office. These also reduce travel costs.

### Financing

All businesses need money to function. This is most often borrowed money which attracts costs such as interest. This again is an ignored area that affects COGS. Even costs, such as raw material holding, warehousing etc. have an impact. Assessing the vendor's financial strength and costs that he incurs in such places are also of significant importance.

Reducing COGS is not an elusive dream, it is easy to execute. One must look at each and every factor that influences COGS and assess them minutely and derive business relevant strategies for their organisations. What's required is - simple rules, clear accountability and some out-of-the-box thinking. And lastly, it's a collaborative effort which needs focus from multiple functions.

There is no right or wrong way to do this. Different business models should focus on different aspects of this and develop a tailored strategy.

CHAPTER 5.7

# Reviews - The Secret of Operational Excellence

Over many years in this industry, a question that has been asked again and again is -

**"What is the secret of operational excellence?"**

The answer to this is very simple:

1. Good planning
2. Robust review mechanism

Any organisation which gets this right is surely on the road to success.

While much is discussed about planning and its impact, we usually do not focus on the importance of review mechanisms. While, in reality, a plan has to be supported by a good review mechanism to ensure smooth flowing of work.

Hence, I have taken up review mechanisms as the topic for the seventh article in this series – '**My sourcing Journal**'.

In this article, I will discuss:

- Importance of planning

- Importance of reviews
- Common mistake in the review process
- Important tenets of a good review
- Reviews at different hierarchical levels
- The outcome of a good review mechanism

As mentioned, operational excellence is nothing but good planning and a robust review mechanism. They are both interdependent elements, which cannot function independently.

### Let's first understand the basis is of good planning.

It is nothing but a **time and action plan**.

T&A is the heart of the sourcing function which keeps everything on track.

A lot of people in the industry go around rubbishing the calendar in the name of changing demand patterns. But the real science is in creating multiple calendars for different requirements rather than a single calendar for the whole organisation. But to try and operate without any calendar is like committing harakiri.

Aligning different stakeholders and calendarising at each milestone, ensures a smooth workflow.

The importance of T&A is discussed in detail in my previous article "*The much-maligned T&A in sourcing*"

While we understand that good planning is the backbone of the sourcing function, the question I ask is - **"Is It Enough?"**

And the simple answer to that question is NO!

For any organisation to understand, if the plan is working or not, it needs to build a good review mechanism.

## Why Are Reviews Important?

As the above graphic highlights - the importance of reviews is immense. They formalise workflow and create a proactive environment.

- With reviews built into the work process, it compels the merchandisers to be **consistent with follow ups**, be it with internal or external stakeholders.
- This consistent follow up leads to timely **identification of issues**, current or future, which may impact the delivery timeline. It helps in timely resolving these issues, ensuring smooth flow of work.
- Any issues which may need senior management intervention are **escalated at the right time**, which helps avoiding last minute firefighting.
- This builds a **proactive environment** where the issues are anticipated and dealt with at the early stages.

I cannot emphasise enough on the merits of a good review mechanism. But the reality is that the reviews, in most cases, are marred by mistakes and are not conducted to extract the benefits stated above.

## What Are The Most Common Mistakes In Review Process?

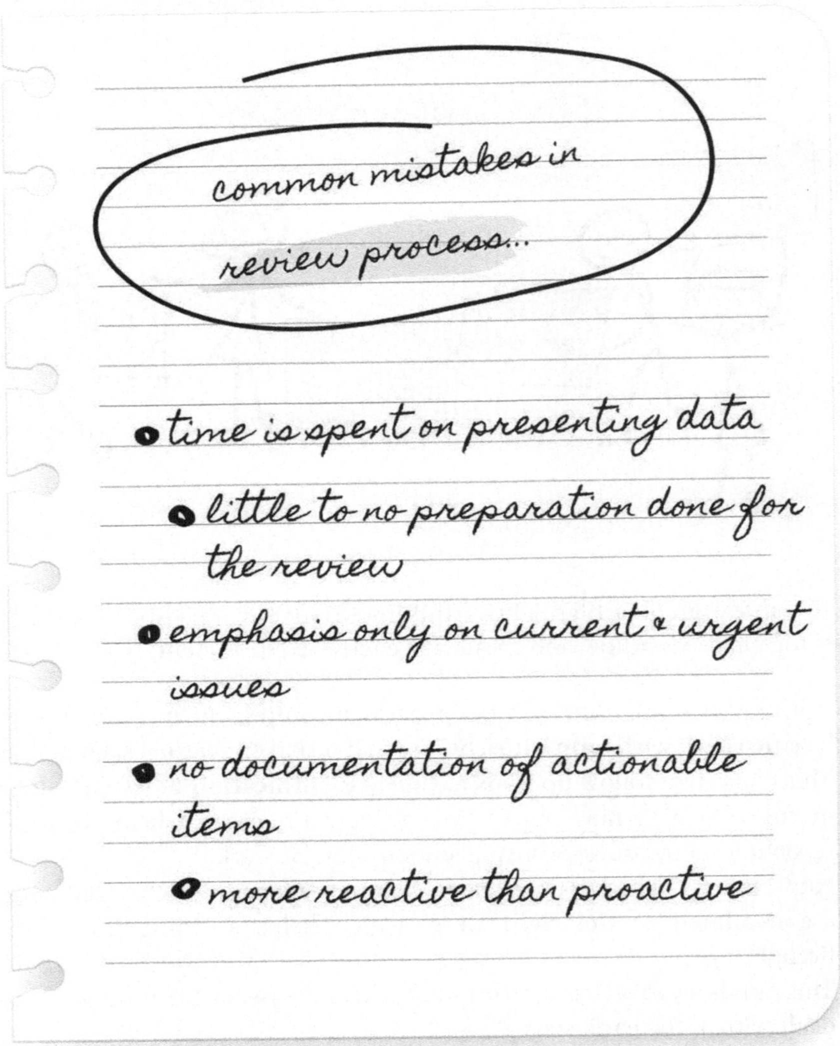


Mostly, during review meetings, the merchants arrive exhausted having spent most of the previous evening, late into the night, calling up factories and other stakeholders to get their data in place. And in the meeting, they take great pride in the correctness of their data.

But when asked to present, they start reading out the data rather than pointing out the red flags and presenting their plan of action for risk mitigation and approval. And they have the most blank expressions when their outcome is challenged. A few probing questions, and meetings become extremely animated and emotional.

**The important thing is to develop a skill in anticipating and pre-empting possible issues and acting well beforehand to ensure that they never arise.**

One should look beyond the 'now' to anticipate future problems. We all spend so much of our time firefighting the issues, which could have been avoided with a futuristic mindset. Planning for tomorrow minimises the problems of today.

The closures discussed in reviews should become action points, which should be documented and circulated to all stakeholders involved. And the next review should start with the updates on the previous actions points, failing which the objective of a review is lost.

A good review is when focus shifts from problem-spotting to problem-solving. There are a few key points one must follow as the pillars of this review process.

## These Tenets Of A Good Review Are:

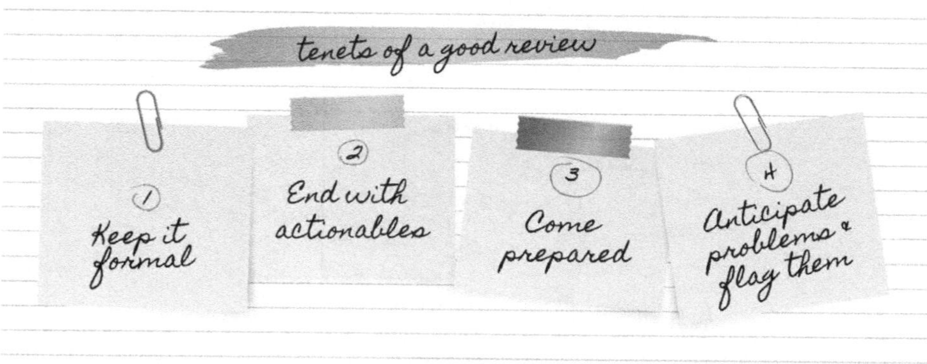


Operational excellence is not an unachievable task. All we need to do is to follow these tenets and ensure that we reap the benefits of a review mechanism.

Many a times, I have noticed that reviews happen only with senior management and the merchants do not follow a process of formal reviews with the vendors or other stakeholders. While, in reality, every level of the hierarchy should be involved in reviews.

In fact, it is the merchants who should spend a large part of their time on reviews with factories and other stakeholders, and managers should spend more time on planning.

One must allocate their time to reviews, meticulously and follow them through.

## Who Should Spend How Much Time On What?

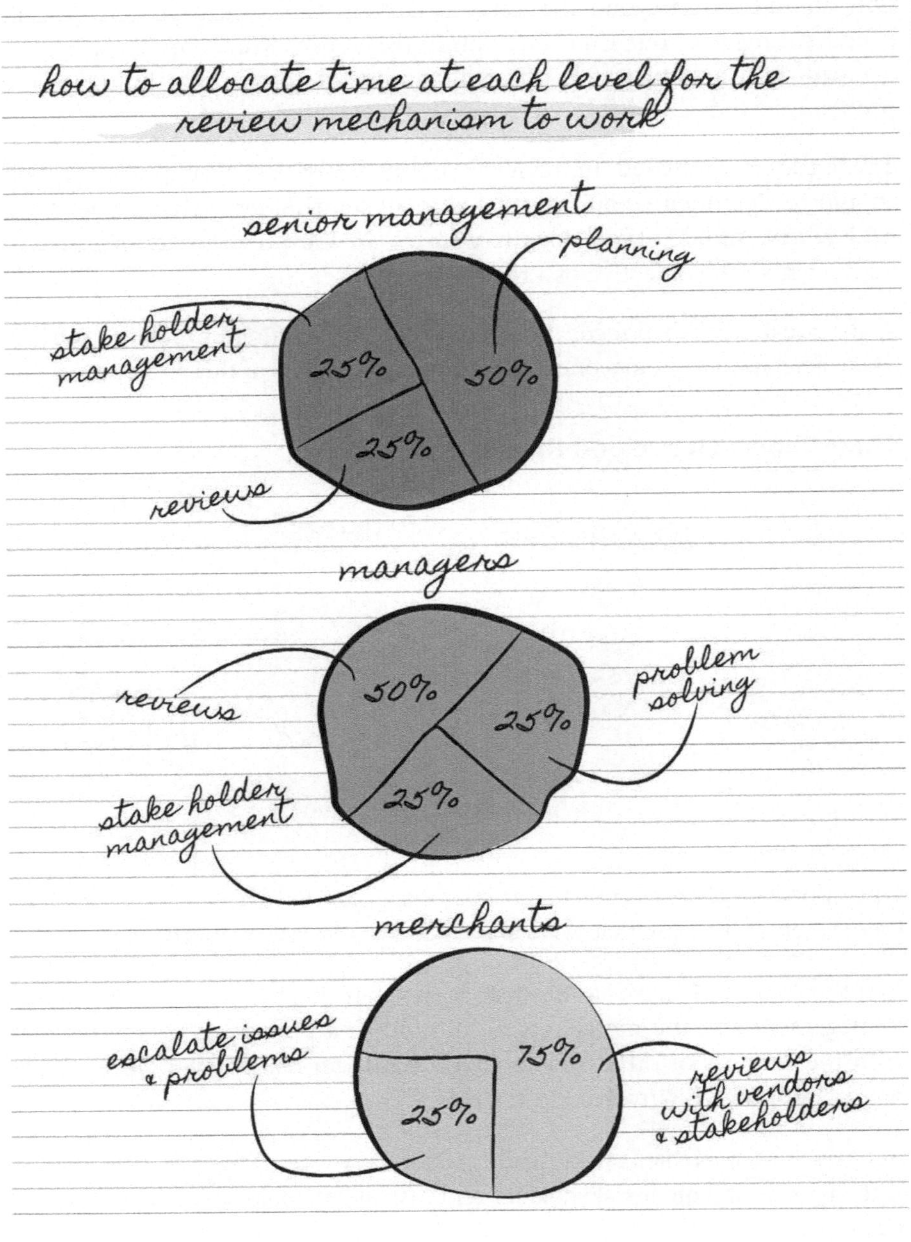

## What Is The Final Outcome Of A Good Review Mechanism?

It ensures that:

- Problems are identified and **red flags** are raised in a timely fashion
- Future problems are anticipated, and **orange flags** are raised months in advance
- Focus is on problem-solving
- It builds a proactive environment in the team

A good review mechanism builds a proactive environment in the team and creates a big impact on the overall business of a company. The actual money lies in anticipating and problem-solving, not firefighting.

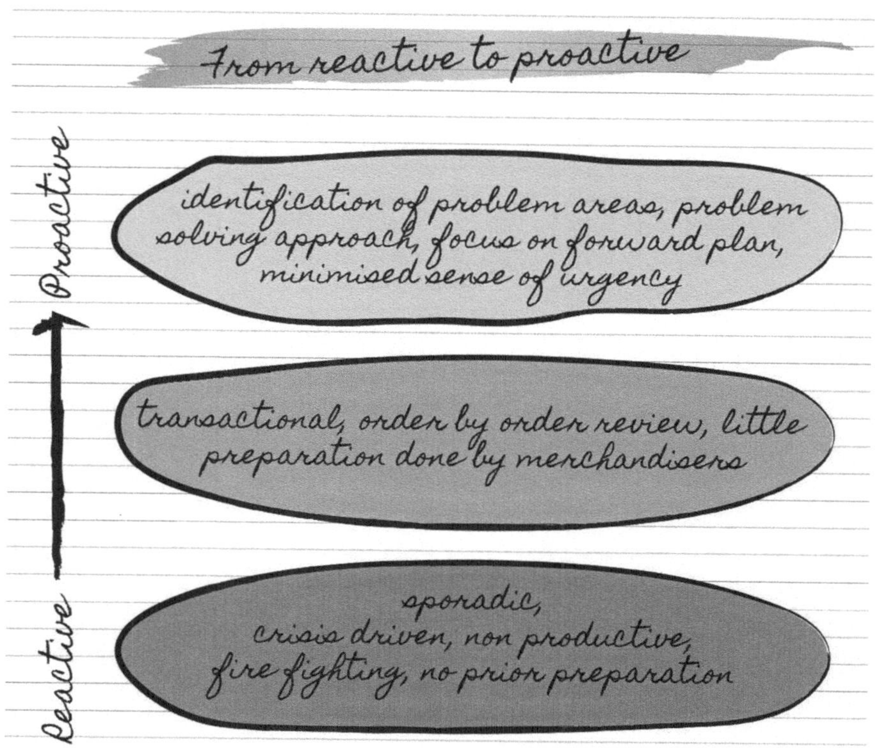


A sourcing leader's job is not to just look at deliveries, but to build a proactive team. The merchandisers need to be conditioned early on in their careers to look at the future and anticipate problems, and then think beyond the ordinary and solve these problems.

**Operational excellence is achieved by anticipating future problems and solving them today.**

We all strive for operational excellence but do little to look beyond obvious. Planning is important but for any plan to work, reviews are the catalyst.

CHAPTER 5.8

# Vendor – How to Be Future Ready?

The most obvious question these days is how to become a preferred vendor in this new emerging market?

I am writing this feature because I was asked this question, during my session in the ASW Marketplace in Dec '20 on **The Future of Sourcing** — 'How to become a preferred vendor?'. It is a very relevant question and one that requires a more detailed discussion.

Vendors are the backbone of the fashion retail industry. It is they who execute the brands' vision and give life to the products. A collaborative union of a brand and a vendor can do wonders in this industry. But how does a vendor become a preferred one?

For this feature, the words '**brand**' and '**retailer**' have been used interchangeably.

Here, I seek answers to this question by dwelling on the following points:

- The basic qualities brands look for in a vendor
- Understanding the evolving requirements of brands
- How should the vendor position his business

Having spent many years in this industry, I have come across many kinds of vendors - big, small, specialised, full-service providers and so on. They all aspire to work with big brands and retailers. While they are able to procure orders for a season or two, many are unable to impress the brand teams and build long-term partnerships.

One may debate about lack of capabilities, infrastructure or high costs as the reasons behind it, but I believe the answer lies elsewhere. They need to demonstrate the four fundamental qualities which are:

## Four Fundamental Qualities Of A Vendor

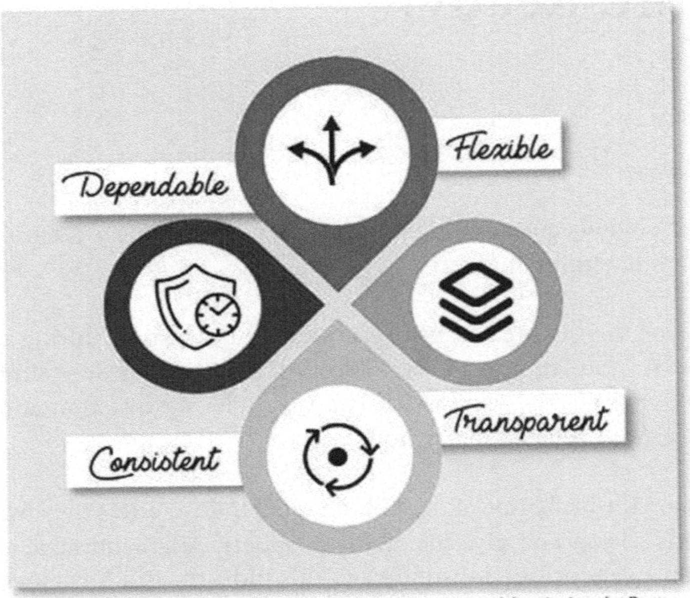


*original infographic created by Aninyda Ray

- **Dependable** – Meeting commitments is the steppingstone of dependability. Vendors, who meet their time-commitments, within cost parameters and requisite quality, are always desired by the brands. They are considered dependable as they don't just deliver the product on time but can be trusted to deliver quality product.
- **Consistent** – '**Every time, on time**', is a mantra every vendor needs to follow. Clubbed with consistency in quality and costs, this becomes the secret of success for many. Many reputed vendors formally brief their customers about this regularly, reiterating their reputation as a consistent performer. This builds trust and reliability, thus helping build a long-term business with them season on season.
- **Transparent** – One of the most important aspects in building trust in business is, transparency. A vendor who is transparent about costing, compliances, dealings with nominated vendors as well as daily/weekly status is always preferred by the brands. They build confidence in the buyers and compel them to work with the vendor again and again.

- **Flexible** – Business, by definition, is dynamic. In many cases, vendor support becomes the need of the hour. This support may vary from holding the goods to reprioritising for early deliveries, reworking commercial terms, changes in shipping instructions or quick turnaround. By extending this support and being flexible, the vendor goes closer to empathising with the brand and their requirement. This building of trust allows the brand/retailer to see the vendor as a partner.

If a vendor is unable to deliver on these **4 fundamental qualities**, it becomes very difficult for them to earn the brand's trust and ensure long-term business.

To move further, we need to understand:

## The Evolving Requirement of Brands

The circumstances today are fast evolving. Businesses are under immense pressure to become more and more efficient. Markets are becoming dynamic, trends are evolving at a much faster pace, go-to market cycles are reduced. In such a scenario, brands are looking for more from the vendors.

Handling smaller volumes with ease, taking on some of brands' inventory pressures, adjustable working in terms of delivery phasing, innovation & design partnership are a few such additional propositions.

And this is where I see as an opportunity for vendors to become the 'preferred' ones. So, how should a vendor approach this opportunity? It is by positioning his business properly?

So, we now come to:

## How should a Vendor position his Business?

In the yesteryears, vendors used to clearly position themselves as – 'Low cost, High Quality' or 'Specialist Vendors' and some vendors and agents used to position themselves as 'Design and Development Partners'. But are these positions sustainable? For a few years maybe, but as brands keep evolving, this will change.

In this fast-evolving market, the dynamics of what brands are looking for is changing. A simple way of looking at it is by positioning himself either as a **Flexible Vendor** or a **Value-Add Vendor**. The graphic below throws light on what this really means for a vendor.

# Vendor Positioning

## Flexible Vendors

**Today**

- Push for high volumes to get efficiences & low costs.
- Focus on operational efficiencies to bring down costs.
- Employ minimum staff, sometimes not even QMS.

**Tomorrow**

- Invest in technologies & processes which allows them to work with very small lots with quick turnaround speed.
- Digitise internal processes & QMS to enable distance quality management & transparency.
- Relook at investments required to offer inventory support & flexibility.

**Value Proposition**

- LOW COST
- SMALL LOT SIZE
- QUICK REPLENISHMENT
- VENDOR MANAGED INVENTORY

## Value Add Vendors

**Today**

- Focus on innovation, new raw material, washes, technical support to brand design & product teams.
- Offer both small lots & large volumes based on price & relationship with the brand.

**Tomorrow**

- Employ design teams to provide fashion & trend solutions along with technical support to the brands.
- Invest in technologies & processes to provide innovation to the brand partners.
- Focus on 3D design, virtual sampling and Line presentations to increase speed to market.

**Value Proposition**

- FASHION CONSULTANT
- QUICK TO MARKET ON TRENDS
- INNOVATION PARTNER

*original infographic created by Aninyda Ray

Vendor needs to develop a positioning strategy. The first step in doing so, is to understand what his brand's business is and how is the brand looking at his factory. Then he needs to understand where he can position himself and accordingly, deliver. He needs to answer what is beyond the fundamental requirements that he is offering to the brand:

- Is he becoming an innovation partner or
- a trend translator and design partner?
- Is he taking some of the brands inventory pressures or
- Is he reducing his working capital requirements?
- Is he supporting with shorter lead times or
- Is he managing demand pull based production?

I would simply suggest that vendors need to look beyond just cost and design to become brands on their own - trusted for their commitments and valued for what they bring on board for their brand partners.

Today, businesses are looking at vendors, who mirror them and work hand-in-hand with them. Gone are the days where the relationship was of a customer and a buyer. Today, it is about partnership and collaboration. A vendor, who can become a true collaborator, is the one who will become a 'preferred' vendor.

## SUPPLIER RELATIONSHIP MANAGEMENT - KEY TO SUCCESS

*"Very well-articulated. Supplier Relationship Management is the key to success for both, the brand, and the business partners/suppliers. It's also very important how do we classify and* ***reward our business partners in terms of their performance considering both hard and soft skills****. I also felt that Sustainability initiatives should also be considered while a supplier selection is being done alongside capacity, capability, willingness, investment and growth, quality etc."*

- Sairam Sharma, DGM Sourcing, Arvind Fashions Limited

## PARTNERS IN PROGRESS

*"Sourcing and vendor selection is equally a commonsense approach. It is a relationship where vendor & brand or retailer, over the period, supplement each other and become partners in progress.*

*A person with right attitude is the biggest and most important deciding factor and I suppose such entity can always be cultivated to be a reliable & long-term vendor – gradually other supporting pillars can always be created with intelligent nurturing and regular support.*

*Indian value system largely gives importance to an element of trust or* ***BHAROSA & PURANA SAMBANDH which plays a big role in uninterrupted supply chain*** *and it's mutual.*

*India's consumption story is a real one and very few factories with scale and understanding of the business brands need to create sustainable supply base to stay relevant and profitable".*

- Paresh shah

## IDEAL COLLABORATOR CHARACTERISTICS

*"I recently went through a program* ***"Become conducted by Kaospilot, Denmark'****. They asked us to do an exercise of finding ideal collaborator characteristics. This was a very interesting exercise where I looked at colleagues I have worked with as well as my clients and other collaborators.*

*Very interestingly this led to looking at things that are tacit and not explicit. My list was:*

*1. Attitude of giving more than taking*

*2. Connectedness to a larger cause*

*3. Mutual respect and trust 4. Having deeper personal connect than just being a collaborator in a task 5. Wisdom and continuous quest for learning*

*This list made sense to me because this is what I stand for. Hence, I believe that alignment in terms of deeper principles and values are far more important in choosing any collaborator – be it a vendor or even customer!"*

- Raja Chidambaram

## SIMPLIFIED PROTOCOLS ARE THE KEY

*"The weight of over adventurism could be a real drag. Weaving the ecosystem around simplified protocols should add to the success".*

- Prashant Kumar, General Manager - Technical Services & QA, Pantaloons

## A DATA DRIVEN DECISION MAKING

*"Interesting article and something which is a real problem in our industry. The more **data driven the decision-making is, the cleaner and transparent the sourcing setup will be**. Constant benchmarking of prices is also important to ensure such problems are caught quickly".*

- Gunish Jain (CEO, Bluekaktus)

## BEST PRACTICES - A TOP-DOWN APPROACH

*"It's high time to make changes in the structure and processes as suggested by you to ensure integrity is intact and served with honesty and perseverance of following best practices as a Top-down approach.*

*Also, would like to mention the **sense of achievement and the respect such a person generates from co-workers** and people he/she is dealing with. They become friends for life and a great support system like a family in the workspace!!!"*

- Sarika Arora, Head Corporate Sales at Royal Data Matics Pvt. Ltd.

## TNA - FREE MIND

*"Throughout my sourcing career, **TNA was my best buddy**. Can"t emphasise how well it fares in pooling/managing the data and keeps mind free from working data clutter. Apparently, brain can be utilised for other cognitive processes like decision making".*

- Soumya Nair

## SIMPLE THINGS ARE THE DIFFICULT ONES

*"While TNA is the most efficient tool, it is time-consuming, and one needs to be patient enough to update at regular intervals. As it is said the simplest things are the difficult ones to do and adopt.*

***When the Business head or the management is serious about TNA and they review regularly, then every merchant would update****. Initially, a merchant would feel the tool is cumbersome and a waste of time, but once he adopts it in his routine, he will find the real benefit of it".*

- Prashanth HV, Product Strategy, Royal Enfield Apparel

## BUILD REGIONAL CHAMPIONS

*"'Decentralization' is always the key to success BUT lot of sincere efforts need to be put in to* ***build 'champions' who would own up region wise 'spokes' and run non-stop like a well-oiled machine,*** *day in and day out, independently, thereby being the CORE DRIVERS/PILLARS of entire supply chain".*

- BS Prasad Apparel Specialist, Consultant – Continuous Improvement / SCQM and Entrepreneur

## A HUB AND SPOKE MODEL

*"Fortunately, during my past work experience, I have been part of Hub and the Spoke Model, and it works wonderfully. Ensuring you are getting the best product at the best cost as various Spoke`s, besides sourcing what is the niche of the region, also compete against each other in* ***cost competitiveness and timely delivery.***

*And of course, it comes with the right amount of empowerment to the regional teams".*

- Sarika Arora, Head Corporate Sales at Royal Data Matics Pvt. Ltd.

## AN INDUSTRY AGNOSTIC PRINCIPLE

*"In my opinion, this is equally applicable across all the industries, of course, in different versions, but the principle remains same.*

***Costing, direct or indirect, does impact the end user, the customer****. Therefore, every organisation should look at how this factor can be looked at, holistically, in a manner that the end user gets the resultant benefit.*

*Having said so, my own observation is that corporates or organisations are not transparent in their financial dealings, be it contracts, bidding process or even routine purchases. There are no standardised processes to monitor this important aspect. Vendor favouritism is the norm of the day and is readily accepted, without any question, thus directly impacting and jeopardising the profits/savings. Though, this is another point of discussion but is also interlinked and therefore, worth pondering".*

- Wing Commander RD Deshpande (Retired), Learning and Development at BYJU'S

## PASSING ON VS TAKING OUT

*"It's interesting to note the difference between 'passing on' a specific cost down the value chain and 'taking out' a specific cost out of the value chain that will, in real terms, be beneficial to the real end consumer".*

- Gaurav Kumar, Head - India Procurement at Compass

## INDUSTRIAL ENGINEERING TEAMS ASSESSMENT

*"As part of support to the sourcing teams in defining cost accuracy can be done by partnering with the industrial engineering teams.* ***The IE teams can assess, evaluate and provide in-depth analysis on the entire cost structure of a production unit like cost per minute and efficiencies which the production unit generally work on.*** *This will help the sourcing teams decide and select on the production unit as well as on the product capability front of the production unit/business partners. Another theory to establish with the design teams while working on COGS is to have a consolidated COGS% for the season. This will help sourcing teams to average out the costs on an overall product basket".*

- Sairam Sharma, DGM Sourcing, Arvind Fashions Limited

## LONG TERM COST IMPACT OF PROCESSES

*"Great ideas! Would like to add another element – the sourcing process. Very often we build processes – which are checks and balances, without realising the implication it has on long term costs. I have often used this example – imaging if you had a vendor base where for all styles, no fit approval process was required. How much saving does it give you in terms of cost and lead time?* ***Investing in improving vendor factory processes*** *and working with building factories with greater capabilities really helps in reducing overall costs. So, taking up pilot projects with vendors really helps. The Quality team should be focused on this".*

- Gunish Jain (CEO, Bluekaktus)

## LEVERAGE TECHNOLOGY

*"It is very important for individual contributors (merchants) to be able to leverage technology to view insights from data rather than running after collating the data and cleaning the data so that it is in presentable form. The organisation should* ***empower the team with the latest tools*** *rather than depending on the excel sheets. And the tool should be accepted throughout the organisation.*

*Also, the day of the review meeting with the individual contributors is very important. Whether it is on the first day or the last day of the working week. I believe the review meet with individual contributors should be on the last day of the working week so that they don't lose the precious weekend to unwind".*

- Mehul

## ANONYMOUS FEEDBACK

*"Key point is Review and the sub point is Practice team/environment.*

*The basis of review mentioned in the article is like walking in a cul-de-sac.*

*The boss is doing a review based on the data available but what about the proactive team and environment building? How is this taken into account?*

*The best way is to get the* ***anonymous feedback from the other parties involved– the fabric suppliers, the trim suppliers, the factories, the logistics and the finance.***

*Each of them will give a true picture of a person, how well he tackled the problems and how much realistic money he saved for the company.*

*This will be true proactive team and environment building which will help the company to grow".*

- Sanjay Lal, Co-founder, Sash Exports (Buying House)

### Conclusion

Sourcing is one of the most important pillars of the apparel industry, and implementing best practices and innovating processes, is of utmost importance. More so, in this era of change and upheaval.

These articles and comments have shed light on various aspects of the sourcing function and compelled us to think differently, strategically and with a future perspective.

Our readers have made the discussion fruitful with exciting insights into this subject.

# Afterword

There are many more learnings to write about, many more anecdotes to share. But for now, this is where I rest my pen…

But I want to leave everyone with some thoughts and a few case studies of brands which broke the mould and created new age successes.

For we can all learn from them…

## CASE STUDY ON ZARA: A CAPITALISTIC FAIRY TALE

Let's take one example of a fashion giant to understand the survival techniques of the fashion houses and their rise to glorious echelons, within the shortest possible time frame.

Lessons learnt from the whopper brand Zara's sustainability would be helpful, since the company's history says, it has not incurred loss for the last 19 years till the recent pandemic happened which had of course crippled majority of the industries in a flash.

Business lessons from the 15-year-old Amancio Ortega Gaona, a school drop-out, the founder of the chain of Zara, would be a worthwhile study case. Amancio, after dropping out from school, pursued trivial job opportunities for a decade before coming up with the brand - Zara.

In no time at all, Zara became the dominating force in the fashion industry. Zara's humongous success has been an area of interest for fashion experts across the globe. When studied closely, this success was attributed to three major factors. Amacio studied the market carefully and based his business proposition on the three basic principles that catapulted the sales and reach of Zara to a global best.

First,

All human beings, irrespective of their age group, belong to a world of hunger for possessing a brand for status's sake, to be accepted more cordially by the people around and by society, at large. Clothes, that people wear, create a veritable impact in setting a status quotient, especially the age group 20 to 34 are forever conscious about the clothes they wear. These clothes were their identity and instruments of status. Therefore, these areas had very little room for compromise. The masses are ready to spend the extra money, walk the extra mile and give in the extra effort to possess these instruments of status. These clothing items add value to status at any time in the history of clothing.

However, the second most important point about owning these clothes is that the critical value or the status is in no way connected with the quality or utility of the products being sold or bought. For women, there existed only two primary parameters – variety and design. These two factors culminated to equip them to create an impact in their social circle. Badly designed clothes lose importance and have no value as far as showing off is concerned. One important takeaway was that nobody cared for quality or utility, but for fetish. Quality of clothes deepened dull in front of designing innovations and that is where Zara could sweep the market with cheaper but designer products. This trend is true even now. No fashionable soul would agree to wear even a very reputed Manish Malhotra or Ritu Kumar, Tarun Tahiliani or Sabyasachi Mukherjee attire twice in public occasions, even if they have spent a bomb on them.

This second knowhow settled with the inference based on the psyche of the masses who eye the designer clothes. The aim was to reap advantage of the unfulfilled demands of owning the very expensive designer clothing. Those coveted clothes on the mannequins and fashion shows have always been the 'objects of desire', but also have remained far out of reach. This sentiment was banked on and effectively cashed on by designing much cheaper but updated garments.

Thirdly, the masses have always been extremely fascinated by reel-life celebrities – Marilyn Monroe of yesteryears to Audrey Hepburn and the modern age power dressers of the likes of Rihanna, Cher, Zendaya, Dua Lipa, Harry Styles and Jennifer Lopez. Once a celebrity catches the fancy of the media, millions of youngsters join the brigade by trying to look chic and more socially accepted through imitation of the celebrity styles. Keeping this dynamism in mind, the waves of the rapid changes in the fashion industry had been tuned to adapt to the times.

An agile supply chain was based on these three insights.

Medium quality material was procured in bulk, research on trends and tendencies were carried out extensively, and trends that have been doing well at premium outlets were prioritised. The influence of pop culture was also not to be ignored in recent decades. A hurried chain of picking designs, getting them ready by local tailors and putting them up in the stores in the shortest possible time gave Zara a headway in the competitive scenario.

Some other band war methodologies include cheaper rates compared to other premium brands and releasing new designs every week. This gave way to three to four times customer footfall in the stores across. To further lure the microcosm of fashion ambassadors, attractive discounts served as a booster. The golden equation between just-in-time production and just-in-case consumption was effectively maintained. Zara releases at least 12,000 designs a year compared to 2000 to 3000 designs of other fashion brands. This well-calculated mechanism took the company to soaring heights of making it a 13 billion-dollar company with 2000 stores spread across 88 countries, approximately.

## Catching the consumer's eye is the need of the day.

Keeping pace with changing tastes and consumer demand has become the business motto. The industry is reeling under the demanding curve of expectations versus supply chain management. Meeting consumer demand is the backbone of the industry and each and every decision can make or break the business mechanics. Let's take a closer look at the nuances of the fashion industry and why it makes such an interesting topic across the globe, unintimidated by race, religion, age, gender or geography.

## A Unique Zara Model That Could Never Be Replicated

First mile strategy was absolutely in place and key players behind *Zara*'s astronomical success, with new initiatives and new narratives that orchestrated fresh moments of change. Let's see the interesting way it churned this success story for the brand. Zara employed a unique market strategy so long unknown and untried by other brands. What Zara did was to standardise some eight or nine types of fabrics and played around with the same fabrics. They customised every design by the innovative use of different silhouettes, putting different prints on it, tweaking around with a combination of the same fabrics.

One fundamental strategy was to hold the raw material in stock, that allowed them to move very fast, and, of course, ahead of their competitors. This tactic was based on the principle of engineering the supply chain at the very beginning of the supply chain. They do add special flavours and design some unique products to attract additional attention of the customers but that's for niche consumerism.

They researched, estimated and responded to market demand and that made their retail stores quite empowered. Zara studied demand very sincerely, and strategically made less than the market demand. The fact that they never made enough, and kept on adding fresh styles almost every week, made customers feel left out if they did not immediately purchase what they liked. Maybe the following week when customers re-visited the store, they found that the designs they had shortlisted or made up their minds to buy were all sold out. Thus, Zara did not give the customers time to ponder, wait & watch, and the fashion-conscious populace grabbed whatever they liked at the very first go. Amancio Ortega Gaona invented this strategy some thirty years ago and developed the concept dramatically to bring about a sustainable global growth for the brand.

They kept the scarcity in demand fuelled and the styles running. Let's say the style of 'puffed sleeves' in women was in, and let's also assume that the colour black was in. What Zara would then do is to create various designs in solid black with puffed sleeves. But they would again produce less than what the market demanded. Next time, when you were at the store, you would have noticed that puffed sleeves are still in but instead of solid black they have now reverted to printed black. And moreover, the solid black would have all sold out. Thus, they made people walk the extra mile to reach the stores. People had to go the shop to buy the latest design on display, almost every week or every fortnight.

This concept is majorly dependent on the backend. The demand is studied, and the product is designed and put out for people to buy. Thus, Zara dictated people's choices. The birth of fast fashion started off with Zara. The model is widely known all over the world. Zara's success inspired many fast companies in Spain to get into the race, but sadly, they never could keep up. All major business schools have case studies on Zara. They have white papers on its business model. Thus, for thirty long years, people knew what to do but they never could copy the model successfully.

Hail Zara! The pathbreaker into the realm of Fast-Fashion.

## ASOS AND BOOHOO CASE STUDY

ASOS and Boohoo are epitomes of remarkable growth in the fashion industry. ASOS stands for 'AsSeenOnScreen' with the clear message to the customers, 'Buy what you see on film and TV'. ASOS sold exclusive imitations of clothing that appeared on screen, big and small. Brad Pitt's 'red leather jacket' from the movie *Fight Club* (1999) is a classic example. Founded in 2000, this British online clothing, accessories, shoes and beauty products retailer targeted the young adults. With a whopping more than 850 brands under its umbrella, and a team of efficient creative retouches delivering advanced image editing and product matching, ASOS was the go-to fashion point from wherever you are located across the globe.

Boohoo was established in 2006 in the United Kingdom and is a leading online fashion group. It showcases an incredible portfolio of 13 market-leading brands, that comprises items of clothing, shoes, accessories and beauty. It has successfully reached millions of customers across the globe.

These companies brought in extraordinary innovation in process and thinking to orchestrate their immaculate success story! The 'Dotcom boom' happened during the late 1900's and early 2000's. As a result of this struggling phase, few companies could survive and the companies that did, thrived, such as Amazon, which is a product of the Dotcom boom. While the other big entities such as Zara were thriving on the first-mile strategy, the new-age companies were focusing on the last-mile strategy.

Their business model was completely based on warehousing and logistics and the efforts were concentrated on getting the product to the consumer at their doorstep. Unlike Zara, that targets people and compels them to step into their showrooms, Amazon had been perfecting their reach to the consumers for over a period through a different approach. Their model was based on putting up as many products as possible on the website, with infinite variety and selling whatever they could, which came to be depicted by the terminology — last-mile strategy. The tech disruption that happened with endless Isles, which translated to putting up as many products as you like on the web, broke the whole retail chain. As a result, the companies that were based primarily on forecasting methodology, started losing out on sales. They failed to understand the new and fast spreading industry trend.

ASOS turns their stylists into social media influencers. The YouTube channel of ASOS has almost 70,000 subscribers and more than 1,000 videos. Their Instagram accounts each have more than 4 million followers. They are thinking ahead of incorporating buy-buttons on social media sites such as Pinterest, Instagram and Facebook Messenger.

Talking of Boohoo, pitted against its competitors, it has a USP. Instead of simply showcasing the product images, they go one step ahead by playing a video of a model wearing the product to give its customers a better idea of how they will look wearing it.

Likewise, Boohoo following similar steps has 7.4 million followers on Instagram and 1.7 million followers on BooHoo Man as of April 2021. They have a decent LinkedIn account, and they update their website regularly. They engage in active email marketing and host an original chapter with attractive content for target customer base. Utilizing the social media, to reach its customer base, has been a common strategy for both companies.

Amazon was thus a forerunner in breaking the chain and very soon it was followed by other companies such as Boohoo and ASOS. They came out with the concept of making very little products and sometimes no product at all and creating virtual products or 3D products to be put up on social media. These brands had a wide range of social influencers working for them and many social media platforms. They were into the mode of manufacturing products based on customer response. Let's say, there were 100 likes on a product, they go and produce 50 such items and, effectively, sell them. If that sells, they make another 100 products and so on. When people stopped liking the product or buying the product or when sales started going down, they stopped producing those items.

This model completely defeated the concept of forecasting. You put out a product and check out whether people like it or not or how many people like it and then you go backward and create that product. This is what is known as the 'Test and Repeat Model', which is a very clear FMCG model.

**The seven P's of ASOS marketing mix are:**

1. Products – Wide variety of products made by ASOS or collaborated brands
2. Price – Affordable price
3. Place - Internet-based platform delivering at the registered addresses
4. Promotion - Website, mobile app, magazines and social networking sites
5. People – Web-based company with fewer employees and thus less man management and costs
6. Process – Online portal displaying a huge variety of products
7. Physical evidence parameter – Easy-to-use mobile and app and website

This was a huge twist in the fashion industry tale and innumerable companies started to put this into practice. A lot of manufacturers, who earlier did not have access to the market, now started accessing products through the online channels. People now started buying through these online channels and stopped visiting the retail stores, hampering the spray & pray method of the earlier years. These companies were slowly dying out. These new tech companies were, on the other hand, not even aware of how majorly they were influencing the buying mechanism and habits of the consumers. Herein, came into the picture companies such as ASOS and BOOHOO, and more recently, Shein. They revolutionised the whole game of the fashion market.

We shall see how Shein did this in a subsequent case study.

## SHIEN CASE STUDY

The Chinese fashion brand, Shien made the headlines by conquering the west through its brilliant market strategy. The aggressive pace at which Shien became the largest cross-border fast-fashion, e-commerce company in the world makes for an insightful case study. It has spread its reach across more than 200 countries, including the United States, France, Russia and Germany. Studies show that the Shien app had more than 177 million downloads in 2021 and had more than 43.7 million clients. Shien had more than 10 million monthly active users in the US alone. Its annual revenue in 2021 is believed to have exceeded $16 billion USD, which was a straight jump from $10 billion in 2020.

Shien was founded in 2008, as a B2C Chinese online clothing and accessories retailer selling worldwide, outside China. It has clothing for men, women and children of all sizes, suited for all occasions. It also includes home life products. Not much is known about Chrs Xu, Shien's founder, who is said to be a Chinese American graduate from Washington University or maybe from Qingdao University, as heard from various sources.

Shien, as a part of its marketing strategy, has no permanent brick-and-mortar stores. But it has opened temporary pop-up stores in the big and happening cities such as Madrid, Melbourne, Las Vegas, Milan and Barcelona that include social media friendly spots, where we find customers eagerly hogging the limelight and getting clicked for social media, while enjoying shopping.

Shien's business model targets the western gen-z consumer base; and as Google trends indicate, US-based netizens look up for the brand Shien three times more than their western counterparts such as Zara, Boohoo and H&M.

Shien's real-time fast-fashion model is extremely quick to identify fashion trends and continuously strives to have minimum manufacturing cycles. To achieve trends identification, designing, manufacturing and shipping at record time, producing 500-2000 new products every day, Shien uses an in-house design team and comprehensive analysis of fashion trend data.

The speed and frequency of launching new products make it a champion among the fashion frontrunners. In 2020, Shien launched an astonishing 150,000 new items, which comes to approximately 10,000 new items per month. They could reach Zara's annual new product volume in merely a couple of months, and it had grown even faster since then. Records of March 2021 show that Shien produced an average of 2,000 new products per day in the women's clothing category.

Shien sells its products at half the price of its western counterparts and showcases items that are more diverse in terms of colours and patterns. The brand is focused at reaching people even of lower economic strata by offering trendy clothes at very affordable ranges. Shien also believes in the micro-influencer mode of marketing. They give out free products to a handful of followers for posting their products on Instagram and YouTube, among others. Through referral schemes, these followers stand the chance to win 10 to 20% commission too, which is an effective strategy in spreading brand awareness.

Statistics of January 2022 show that 10% of the web traffic to Shien websites were through influencer recommendations, while 45% accounted for reach through organic search results. Direct access traffic of more than 38% indicates that Shien enjoys a very high proportion of returning customers.

After entering the Middle East market in 2016, Shien's sales reached 200 million RMB that same year. Shien enjoys being among the top ten shopping apps in UAE and Saudi Arabia. Shien's footfall in any new country has been remarkably intense.

Shien uses Amazon's strategy of promoting the shopping habits of the West through data collection from search optimization. The company was so well equipped that they could ably compete and even defeat Amazon at its own strategy. American teenagers voted Shien to be the most popular online clothing store in the US. Currently, monthly downloads of Shien exceed that of Amazon. Shien and Amazon have now mutually agreed to incur the benefit of cross-promotion by listing Shien's products on Amazon.

Shien has a catalogue that is easy to navigate with very clearly categorized products based on gender, size, fashion trends, seasonal trends, type of clothing, material and styles. Shien maintains a humongous range of products and keeps on updating its catalogue at short and regular intervals, which keeps customers hooked every time they visit the online stores.

Shien's methodology is perfectly suited for the young and price-aware consumers, who do not need a long-lasting professional wardrobe, rather a huge variety of stylish clothing. Shien has 27.6% customers between the ages of 18 and 24 and 29.2% between 25 and 34. Besides their huge pool of micro-influencers, Shien also collaborates with media personalities, who are adored, imitated and followed by young adults, such as Katy Perry, Lil Nas X, Rita Ora, Nick Jonas and Hailey Bieber.

The pandemic habit of e-buying of the consuming mass gave a huge boost to the brand. People in general had started exploring e-commerce options more during the lockdown phase. They spent much more time browsing and shopping online, which acted as a huge incentive for the newcomers in the industry such as Shien and the brand took very good advantage of it by pushing their sales to dramatic levels.

# Acknowledgements

I believe no lone wolf can ever succeed! And I am very lucky to have friends and colleagues who have supported me and, positively, contributed towards a lot of my learnings.

They have also taken out time, read my chapters and shared their learnings, experiences and insights, making this journey an enriching one.

Some of those insights are shared in this as part of the conclusive chapters. I would like to take this page to thank them all...

I am also grateful to apparel resources who have given me an opportunity to publish my articles on their esteemed website. They have also obliged in permitting me to make those articles a part of this book.

- Sai Navneethan Markandan, Regional Head South Asia Markets, Sustainable Products
- Ajay Ravuri, General Manager Quality, Arvind Fashions Limited
- Akhil Khanna, Managing Director, SRV Knittech Pvt Limited
- BS Prasad Apparel Specialist, Consultant, Continuous Improvement SCQM and Entrepreneur
- Dipin KK
- Garima Joshi, Co- founder Meraki
- Gaurav Kumar, Head - India Procurement at Compass
- Gautam Kotmraju, former Co-founder, CultSport, CultGear
- Gunish Jain, CEO BlueKaktus
- Himanshu Singh, Co- founder, Meraki
- Kamal Gupta, Entrepreneur
- Karunesh Vir Vohra, Catalyst, Business of Design, BO
- Krishna Kumar (KK), IT Entrepreneur and Supply Chain Enthusiast
- Mehul
- Moutushi Dey, Design Consultant

- Neeraj Katoch, Sr. Mgr B&M, Arvind Fashions
- Nithya Easwaran, Managing Director, Multiples Alternate Asset
- Management Pvt Ltd
- Nitin Gupta, Design, Innovation & BD, Arvind Ltd.
- Paresh Shah
- Poonam Sood Lal, Consultant, Co-founder, Sash Exports (Buying House)
- Prasenjit Adhikari, Creative Director Arrow, Arvind brands
- Prashant Kumar, General Manager - Technical Services & QA, Pantaloons
- Prashanth HV, Product Strategy, Royal Enfield Apparel
- Raja Chidambaram
- Rajesh Kumar, VP & Creative Director, US Polo Assn.
- Ram Subramanium, MBA, PMP, Scrum Master, Principal Consultant at Global Channel Solutions Inc
- Ramesh Ramalingam, VP Sourcing Operations, Arvind Fashions
- Ravindra Chawla, Operations Head Quality, Arvind Lifestyle Brands Ltd.
- RP Singh, President, Eveline International
- Rupa Giani, Entrepreneur, Designer, Co-founder Qfamily, Cute and Cool
- Sairam Sharma, DGM Sourcing, Arvind Fashions Limited
- Sandeep Golam, director operations at Denimach Limited
- Sanjay Lal, Co-founder, Sash Exports (Buying House)
- Sarika Arora, Head Corporate Sales, Royal Data Matics Pvt. Ltd.
- Shankar
- Soumya Nair
- Swati Sriram, Design Consultant (Apparel and Home Furnishing)
- Wing Commander RD Deshpande (Retired), Learning and Development at BYJU'S
- Yogesh Agiwal, Founder & CEO - Crossover Leadership Journeys

9 788197 687624

Printed at Repro India Ltd.